MW01538437

HR Fundamentals for Non-HR Managers: Can We Be Friends? (& CYA!)

Love, your HR Team

HR.com
Maximizing Human Potential

Copyright © 2021 by HR.com

Revision Date: 22nd June, 2021

AN INTRODUCTION

Herding cats? As a manager, if you feel this way at times, don't worry! You are in good company —and, with this book, you are in good hands! Especially since the number one reason that people leave a company is because of their manager, namely, YOU! There are a number of responsibilities you have as the manager, some of which you are painfully aware of. And, then there is the "don't know what you don't know" aspect of things—and this is where we can help! When you peruse the Table of Contents of this book, you may see topics and think, "I got this!" But, do you? It's best to look through the chapter to confirm you've not overlooked something important. We guess you could say this book is "like a box of chocolates, because you never know what you're gonna get" (Forrest Gump).

There will certainly be nuggets of truth and helpful tips to identify challenges you currently have (or will someday soon)! Rethinking is the first step to retooling. Even if you are doing everything right, and with excellence, you will still be challenged to look in the mirror to see if there is anything just under the surface, you know... just waiting to erupt! You may wonder how we know this. No, we're not psychics—but we are HR.com! And, we know a thing or two about the stuff that your Human Resources (HR) department wishes you knew or wishes you were doing. How, you ask? Well, we interact with over 1.88 million HR leaders every year. We hope that the knowledge you glean from the upcoming chapters will enhance your partnership with HR and avoid headaches in complying with national, regional, and local labor laws.

Managing a team requires the right collection of tools. You must learn to wield these tools to inspire your team (whether they are remote or face-to-face).

Important tips you will discover in these pages are:

- How to set direction so your employees are focused on the right things

- How to inspire employees so they want to do the right things

- How to hire employees that are capable of doing the right things

- How to develop employees so they continuously get better at doing the right things

- How to work with HR so that you get the benefit of their expertise

- How to work with HR so that they keep you out of trouble with labor legislation

We hope that you will enjoy being provoked (by thoughts), prodded (not like cattle), and propelled (like a rocket launch... the sky's the limit!). More importantly, we hope you will find encouragement that you are not alone. Remember, we all get by with a little help from our friends! And we're in the friend zone here, right? Being the manager has a lot of benefits, but great rewards come with even greater responsibilities. The goal is to equip yourself to better equip and engage your team. And, we are hedging the bets that you will achieve and exceed this goal! There are no promises that this book will change your life, BUT, it can help to optimize the ways you lead your team. So, keep calm, and lead on! What are you waiting for?! Turn the page already!

6

HR Fundamentals for Non-HR Managers: Can We Be Friends? (& CYA!)

TABLE OF CONTENTS

TABLE OF CONTENTS

8

HR Fundamentals for Non-HR Managers: Can We Be Friends? (& CYA!)

TABLE OF CONTENTS

MANAGER TO LEADER

HR for Non-HR Managers

This book is dedicated to two groups of readers:

If you are a non-HR manager who desires to develop as a leader, and inspire your team to maximize their potential while doing so in ways aligned to business and HR best practices - this book was written for you!

It is also dedicated to all HR professionals who are inspiring human potential in their organizations and are responsible for making sure their managers and employees are equipped to be the best they can be while staying out of trouble!

We applaud you for all of the hats you wear, but particularly that of "Coach" for your teams. We are rooting for you!

This book was a collaborative effort by friends and family of HR.com including:

Authors: David Creelman, Mwannesi Wade, Jo Weech, Debbie Hill, Dr. Heidi Scott, Gavin Morton, and Debbie McGrath
Special Contributors: Robin Schooling, Torin Ellis, and Ron Thomas
Editor: Heather Reid
Design: Deepak S, Jason Clavo, Arun Kumar and Shelley Marsland

We remain grateful to everyone who shared in the collaboratively crafted book aimed at inspiring human potential in all organizations across the workforce.

HR Fundamentals for Non HR Managers: Can We Be Friends? (and CYA)
Publication date: March 12, 2021 ISBN: 978-1-7357231-3-6

SECTION 1

Being a Strategic Leader:
Aligning your team with the bigger picture

MISSION, VISION, & VALUES

WHAT'S THE MASTER PLAN?

To align your team with the company's mission, vision, and values, one must first understand what they are.

Key Terms and Definitions

Mission – why we exist and what we aim to accomplish

Vision – what success will look like

Values – what behaviors we commit to as we strive for that success

The Issue

As a manager, you carry the increased responsibilities and exposures that come with the role. If research is correct (and we bet it is!), YOU are the number one reason why people will either stay in or leave their jobs! Whoa, that's a lot to process.

Your company's mission, vision, and values statements can play a role in helping to inspire and retain your employees. People like to know they are part of something bigger; the mission, vision, and values show what the bigger thing is.

12

HR Fundamentals for Non-HR Managers: Can We Be Friends? (& CYA!)

It's the old story of the traveler stopping by a construction site and talking to two bricklayers. He asked the first one, who was frowning over his work, what he was doing. "I'm laying bricks, can't you see that? It's heavy work." The traveler then asked the second one, who was quite unaccountably smiling while he did the heavy work, what he was doing. The second worker looked up with a charming smile, "I'm building a cathedral."

The mission, vision, and values also help employees make choices that are aligned with the company's purpose. The bricklayer who knows they are part of building a cathedral will make different choices about how much care is required in placing a brick than the one who feels they are just building a wall.

In a sense, all of the company's culture should be a reflection and a manifestation of the company's mission, vision, and values. Your job as a manager is to make the connections so that employees understand and buy in to the mission, vision, and values. If you do that well, it will create the culture you want and you need.

A Short Story

Nia is the manager of a newly assembled team at her company. They are in the business of creating posters, pens, travel mugs and the like with inspirational messaging. In order to transition herself and her team into their new roles, she has decided to host a special meeting to align everyone with the company's mission.

Section 1 • Chapter 1 • Mission, Vision, & Values: What's the master plan?

13

Nia: OK, everyone, it's important you buy into the company mission, so let's spend 20 minutes getting that nailed down before we move on to the next agenda item. Ahmed, what do you think about the company mission?

Ahmed: I didn't know we had a mission.

Tyler: I'm pretty sure we do. I saw it on a poster somewhere.

Nia: Okay, Tyler then you start. How do you feel about the company mission?

Tyler: I saw the poster, but I don't remember it. Maybe I can look it up and get back to you.

Nia: No, no, no. We're doing this now. Let me read it out. The first line is "We bring out the best in people by reminding them of their own best qualities." Sung, how do you feel about that.

Sung: It's nice. It's pretty.

Nia: Yes, but what I want is to know how you feel about it in terms of your own job.

Sung: Oh, it's got nothing to do with me. I just worry about tracking inventory.

Ahmed: In any case, shouldn't the mission be about treating each other with respect?

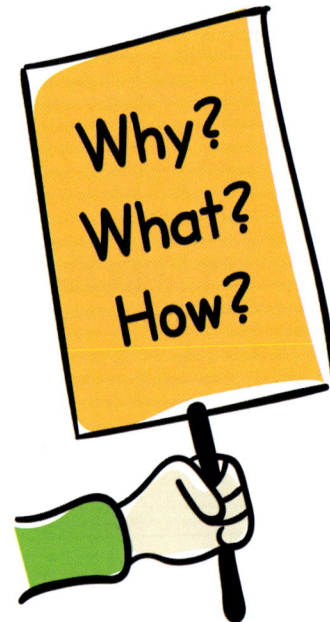

Nia: Ahmed, that's important but it's a value not a mission.

Ahmed: What's the difference?

Nia: (sighs) I don't think we're going to get this done in 20 minutes.

What We Mean by Mission, Vision, and Values

Mission, vision and value statements are usually pretty straightforward but as Nia discovered in that short story, employees often don't know what they are or why it matters to them. It's your role as a manager to make sure employees do know your company's mission and even more importantly understand their role in bringing the mission, vision, and values to life.

First, let's be clear; the meanings of the terms mission, vision, and value are often unclear. (Did that make sense?) What we're trying to say is that different companies use these words in different ways, and some throw in additional words like "purpose" which can add to the

> Inspiring, well-run companies are considered "great places to work" because their employees are aligned to the mission, vision, and values.

Let's take a look at the real example of Southwest Airlines, a company that is consistently rated as one of the best places to work and one of the only airlines to never lay off employees or lose money. Here are their Mission, Vision, and Values statements:

Mission: The mission of Southwest Airlines is dedication to the highest quality of Customer Service delivered with a sense of warmth, friendliness, individual pride, and Company Spirit.

Vision: To become the world's most loved, most flown, and most profitable airline

confusion. We will explain our approach to mission, vision, and values; however, what matters is making sure that your employees have a common understanding of the bigger picture. Worry about the end result, not debating the fine points of the definitions.

Here is how we'll define these terms:

- Mission – why we exist and what we aim to accomplish

- Vision – what success will look like

- Values – what behaviors we commit to as we strive for that success

Section 1 • Chapter 1 • Mission, Vision, & Values: What's the master plan?

15

Why ? Who

Mission - why we exist and what we aim to accomplish

Values:

- Live the Southwest Way
- Warrior Spirit
- Servant's Heart
- Fun-LUVing Attitude
- Work the Southwest Way
- Safety and Reliability
- Friendly Customer Service
- Low Costs [1]

Packs a punch, doesn't it? Impactful because the words are few but powerful. Does it make you want to join Southwest? If you were a Southwest employee, would this guide how you approach your own work? If so, that's a good mission statement.

You may not have a chance to be involved in crafting your company's mission, vision, and values statements, however an example like Southwest's shows what you ought to be pulling out of them. Even if your own company's statements are not as vibrant as Southwest's, you should try to bring them to life as you explain them to your team. Give an example of something an employee or the department as a whole might do that would _not_ align with the mission, vision, and values. Contrast that with an example of something that WOULD align. Ask them to come up with their own examples. Then discuss some of the things you've seen employees do—even if they are small things—that align with the mission, vision, or values.

> Alignment with the company mission, with a view of the company vision, will help your team achieve success in daily goals.

Let's look at another example. Google's mission is, "To organize the world's information and make it universally accessible and useful." It's clear, concise, ambitious, and unique to Google.

Here's one more set of statements, this time from the Princess Margaret Cancer Centre.

Mission: To raise and steward funds to deliver breakthrough research, exemplary teaching, and compassionate care at The Princess Margaret, one of the top 5 cancer research centres in the world.

Vision: Conquer Cancer in Our Lifetime

Values:
- Passion for the Vision
- Entrepreneurship
- Partnership
- Accountability
- Sustainability [2]

Imagine the receptionist whose job it is to get visitors to fill in the appropriate form versus the one whose job is part of conquering cancer in their lifetime. Ok, you get it now don't you? Even if your company isn't conquering cancer, it *is* delivering something your customers truly value. Make sure your employees understand that.

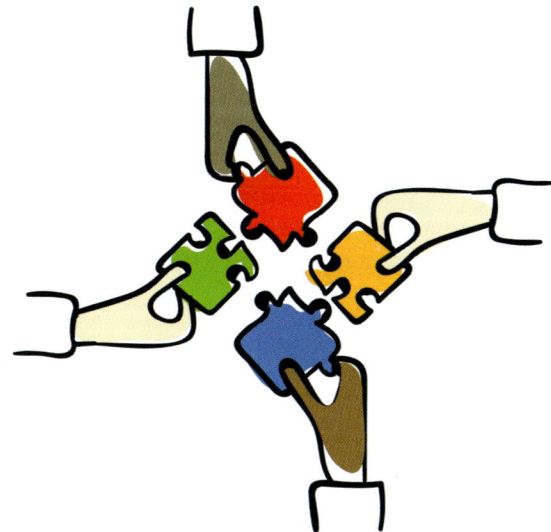

Section 1 • Chapter 1 • Mission, Vision, & Values: What's the master plan?

17

To Get Team Buy-In, Start by Buying in Yourself

We're going to look at mission and vision before we look at values. Whether you are creating your own mission and vision statements or working with the ones you were given, you need to get your team's buy-in. Your team needs to understand and recognize the value of working collectively to achieve the goals of your company. Without your team's support, the company's mission statement becomes meaningless, and more importantly, their responsibilities become less meaningful. As Art Johnson notes in *How to Get Employees to Align with the Company's Mission*,

> "Organizational success is often linked to...clear mission...But without employee buy-in, these concepts are worthless." [3]

The best way to align your team with your company's mission and vision is to make sure they understand the intent behind each statement. That's going to take some thinking on your part,

some thinking on their part, and a fair bit of ongoing discussion so that the connection between the statements and their individual work is clear.

Here is how to start:

Step 1:

Think about what your company's mission and vision mean to you. What part of the intent behind those statements resonates with you? What inspires you? How does it help focus your own goals and activities?

Don't head into a discussion with your team without having answers to those questions first. You want to approach the discussion with a certain amount of passion in your heart; and to have the ability to explain why the mission matters to you before you try to convince your team that it should matter to them.

Focusing On What Makes your Company Different

When you are thinking about your

mission and vision, it's worth pondering what makes you different than your competitors. The mission and vision need to reflect who you are, and at the same time emphasize some of the things that make your organization special.

As Clifton and Harter revealed,

> An organization's performance improves when its employees understand what differentiates its brand. But Gallup analytics reveals that less than half of U.S. employees (41%) strongly agree that they know what their organization stands for and what makes it different from its competitors. [4]

You should work from the assumption that knowing what makes you different is important and that employees may have no clue what those differences are. That's why you were made a manager — to close that gap.

Ideally, the mission and vision statements clearly show some elements of differentiation. If not, then you'll have to extrapolate from what's in those statements. This takes us to your next step.

Step 2:
Think about, and be ready to articulate, how the mission and vision relate to what makes your organization unique.

The Crucial Role of Communication
Whether you are creating your own mission statement or working with the one you were given, you need to effectively communicate it to your team. As Art Johnson notes in *How to Get Employees to Align with the Company's Mission*,

> "Employee engagement is essential to...success, and alignment is arguably even more important... We all know intuitively that communication is critical to driving alignment and success." [5]

The company mission is different from the company vision, but alignment needs to be with both.

Help employees get a clear view of the company vision!

Section 1 • Chapter 1 • Mission, Vision, & Values: What's the master plan?

19

There we have it; it's about communication. Now ask yourself, is putting the mission and vision in a poster on the wall sufficient communication? What about having a meeting where you read them out? What if you go on to explain them?

Steps one and two are good, but they're far from sufficient. Employees need a chance to discuss their ideas. This brings us to steps 3 and 4.

Step 3:

Meet with employees and, bringing your own passion to the discussion, explain what the mission and vision are, why they're important, how it makes the company different from its competitors, and what it means to you personally.

Step 4:

Give employees a chance to discuss these ideas. Break them into small groups of 2-4 people so they get a chance to voice their ideas. Get people to share their best insights with the full team. This can (and should) be done with remote teams as well, video conference technology now allows breakout rooms.

You don't need to do this all at once. You can break up the discussion over several meetings. In fact, you may find that setting aside 15 minutes to discuss various aspects of mission and vision over four meetings, is more effective than a single, one-hour meeting. You should end each meeting with a request that employees think about these ideas so that they can share their reflections in the next discussion.

20

HR Fundamentals for Non-HR Managers: Can We Be Friends? (& CYA!)

> Company culture: the personality of a company. It defines the environment in which employees work and includes a variety of elements: work environment, company mission, values, ethics, expectations.

So, here is what you can do to gently bring along employees who are skeptical about the mission:

- Ask them what makes them proud about the company – discuss how that relates to this mission and vision.

- Ask them why you have repeat customers and what value the company delivers to those customers – discuss how that relates to this mission.

- Talk about their own priorities this year – discuss how that relates to the company's mission and vision.

Remember that the people in your HR department have a lot of expertise in getting employees engaged with new ideas. Talk to them about how to best approach this. Remember that HR can be a great thinking partner; you can bounce around some ideas with them whenever you face people issues.

While this all sounds great, it can be hard to get everyone behind the company mission. Yeah, this is an understatement! Some team members may struggle to fully buy-in to the value of the company mission or could even be disgruntled and less than inclined to support the mission. Of course, there is NO ONE on your team like this, right?

Section 1 • Chapter 1 • Mission, Vision, & Values: What's the master plan?

21

Additional Ways You Can Spur Discussion

Here are some additional questions you can pose to employees to help them get engaged with the mission and vision. Some questions specifically related to the vision include:

- Ask people what they would like to read about the company ten years from now – discuss how that relates to the vision.

- Ask people in what way your company will be seen as different from the competitors in 10 years – discuss how that relates to the vision.

- Talk about some of the corporate priorities this year – discuss how that relates to the vision.

Going Deeper, Making the Connection to their Own Work

In the story about the bricklayer and the cathedral, the worker was able to see how their task contributed to mission and vision. That isn't always the case. It's also true that sometimes it is a long way from an individual's day to day tasks to the grand vision of the whole organization. You do want to make the connection. It's not enough that your team agrees with the mission and vision in principle; they have to see how they are part of it. Here are some tips for doing so:

- As before, start with yourself. Be able to articulate your own connection to the mission before you ask others to articulate theirs.

> Identifying the framework for the company culture can be cross-departmental, but interpreted individually.

> " Realize the culture isn't singular – Cultures exist all throughout your company. There are subcultures and microcultures that happen within departments and between business units. There is no˙one˙ culture which captures all that a company is.[6] "

22

HR Fundamentals for Non-HR Managers: Can We Be Friends? (& CYA!)

- Rather than ask them to make a big leap from their task to the overall mission, start with a discussion of the role the whole department plays; and if you are in a sub-department, show why that sub-department is crucial to the whole department. From there, you are in a position to find the connection as to why their work is crucial to the sub-department.

- As before, let them talk. You lead off with explanations, then let them buy-in to the connection between mission and their own work by putting it in their own words. Encourage them to articulate how what they do helps the organization accomplish what it is after.

> "Culture has a direct measurable impact on performance... One in three employees worldwide strongly agree with the statement 'The mission or purpose of my organization makes me feel my job is important'..."[7]

Section 1 • Chapter 1 • Mission, Vision, & Values: What's the master plan?

23

Finally, through all this, you need to show you care. You need to show that you appreciate how their individual tasks matter to the bigger picture. You need to prove you believe their work matters, or they never will.

"You don't change culture through emails or memos. You change it through relationships… one conversation at a time."
@steelethoughts

Getting Employees to Live the Company's Values

Now on to values. Values are probably the most tangible part of the mission, vision, values trio. They are also the element that is closest to the employees' day to day lives. If you are defining your values, you might take a look back at how Southwest has done it. On their list they include some generic values like safety and customer service, however, what stands out are the values that make them unique such as Warrior Spirit.

"Live and own the culture yourself…There will always be room to evolve, tweak and shift your company's culture because it's ever moving…then culture would come alive and…add more value.[8]

24

HR Fundamentals for Non-HR Managers: Can We Be Friends? (& CYA!)

Some things you can discuss with employees are:

- How are the values we live here different than some other organizations?

- Which of the values matters most to you personally?

- Can you think of an example, where you saw one of your colleagues living a value you feel is important?

You may get the impression that defining or engaging employees with the mission vision and values is a one-time thing—a meeting you can have one Friday afternoon and then forget about it. Quite the contrary. It's up to you as the manager to have mission, vision, and values top of mind and to be continually making the connection for employees between things that are happening now and the mission, vision, and values. Whenever you do something, see if there is a way to show people the connection. Even more important, whenever you see someone living the mission, vision, or values, be sure to show your appreciation for their doing so. For example, praising behavior that demonstrates living the values of the organization often helps all members remain focused on them.

The Link to Culture

When employees are living the mission, vision, and values, they show up in what we often refer to as the company culture. Let's talk about culture for a moment. When a company is at its best, its culture should energize its employees. You don't need power energy drinks to achieve this; it will happen naturally when your employees feel good about your team and your company!

As you probably know, culture, as a concept, can be hard to define. This can include expectations around communication style, dress code, work hours, and daily interactions. Culture is often best defined as "The way we do things around here." The way you do things around your workplace should reflect what you are ultimately trying to achieve (mission and vision) and the values that guide day to day behavior.

Use the mission, vision, and values as guideposts to direct behavior towards the culture you want to establish. As always, this is not a one-off meeting; it's what takes place in the conversations you have with employees every day; it's what behaviors you suggest need to be changed and the behaviors you celebrate. The idea of mission, vision, and values helps you avoid getting so caught in the nitty-gritty of the day to day work, that you lose sight of the bigger picture.

Section 1 • Chapter 1 • Mission, Vision, & Values: What's the master plan?

25

> Don't just tell employees about the desired culture; give them a chance to discuss it in their own words.

Back to the Story

The manager in our story, Nia, underestimated what was involved in gaining agreement on and understanding of the company's mission. It's not a complex topic per se, it's just something that requires ongoing discussion so that employees get clarity about what the mission, vision, and values are. They need to notice how those things show up in their day to day work. It's Nia's job to bring that clarity and create those connections, but she'll have to do so over a period of time.

Summing Up

Let's digest what we've discussed. You can maximize the potential of your team by building a solid foundation, which includes a clearly defined mission, vision, and values that the team understands and buys into. Companies who get this right typically are inspiring places to work. Learn from companies that have already been successful with developing a solid foundation. You can go online right now and look up the mission statement of companies you admire. Speak to your friends in other companies and ask what has worked for them.

Alignment with the company's mission, with a view of the company vision, will help your team reach their daily goals and create the culture you desire.

What are the keys to getting buy-in to mission, vision, and values?

- Start with yourself. Are you clear on how each concept is defined at your company?

- Take the time to explain it to your team, building the explanation on your own personal connection to and passion about the mission, vision, and values.

- Give employees time to discuss these ideas, and don't try to get it all done in one meeting.

Connect the ideas to day to day working life by celebrating the right behaviors, gently correcting the wrong ones, and continually helping people see the connection between their tasks and the bigger picture.

Now, let's move on to an activity that can help you with mission, vision, and values.

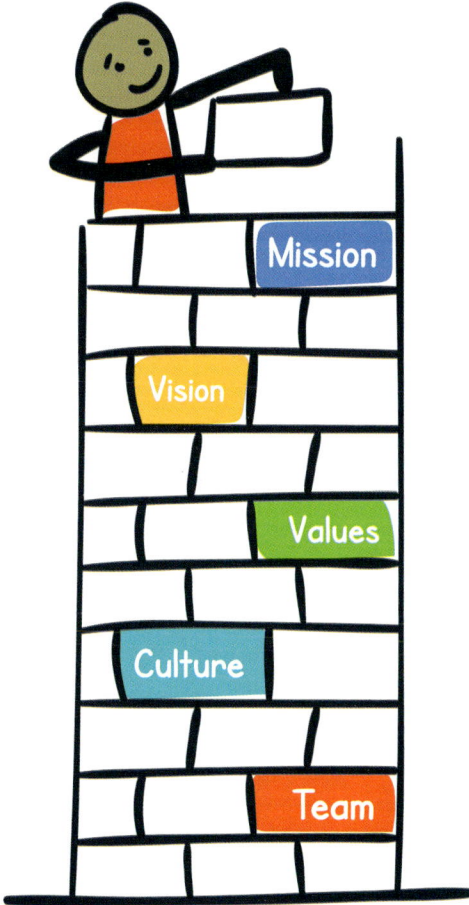

Building Up Your Team: A Company Culture Activity

There are numerous building blocks for you, as the manager, to use to align your team with your company's purpose, mission, vision, and values. As the alignment grows, so will the positive aspects of the team and company cultures. Take a look at some examples below. Then, in the **Describe Activities/Actions** column fill in the actions, activities, plans, and/or processes you can implement on your team to reach the desired outcome for each **Culture Building Block**. You may find the final column useful for documenting your **Actual Outcomes**.

Here are some potential issues you may wish to tackle:

- What aspects of our culture are we proud of?
- What aspects of our culture fall short?
- How do we handle conflict?
- Do team members support one another?
- As a leader am I fair and transparent?
- Mission accomplished or mission stalled?

Section 1 • Chapter 1 • Mission, Vision, & Values: What's the master plan?

27

Culture Building Block	Desired Outcome	Describe Activities /Actions	Actual Outcome
Team Alignment to the Company Mission.	Work activities aligned with what the company does in an excellent and efficient way.		Example: Once team members fully "bought in," sales increased by 18%.
Team Alignment to the Company's Vision.	Clarifying what it is and asking each team member how their role impacts success.		Example: An employee suggested a change in a form when they realized it created extra work for customers.
Conduct individual and team tasks while embracing company values.	Defining the values, understand how each person interprets those values, and drafting commitment statements to work in alignment with the values.		Conflict was reduced significantly, collaboration was respectfully and equitably executed across the team.

28

HR Fundamentals for Non-HR Managers: Can We Be Friends? (& CYA!)

Culture Building Block	Desired Outcome	Describe Activities /Actions	Actual Outcome
Positive aspects of the culture enhanced and honed.	Regular five minute one on ones to be between all supervisors and team members.		Every team member loved the accountability and the ability to immediately course correct, which enhanced productivity and reduced misunderstandings of the tasks.
Negative aspects of the culture identified and eradicated.	Favoritism being shown towards manager's long-time friends.		Manager stopped spending more business and social time with his old friends and treated all employees equally. Employee engagement improved as everyone experienced fairness and support.

ALIGNING YOUR TEAM WITH THE STRATEGY

BASICS THAT MAKE YOU A BETTER MANAGER

> Strategic alignment of your team first starts with aligning yourself to the company objectives.

Key Terms and Definitions

Strategic Alignment - ensuring your team's goal directly supports the company's strategy

Two-way feedback - giving AND receiving feedback (with humility)

Ongoing feedback - giving frequent informal feedback

Constructive feedback - specific fact-based feedback an employee can act on

Sandwich feedback - praise, opportunity for improvement, praise.

The Issue

In chapter 1 we looked at the guiding principles of mission, vision, and values. Now we need to look at a variety of tools and ideas that will help you keep your team aligned with those high-level goals.

A Short Story

Charles is the Vice President of Operations for a manufacturing company. He manages what feels like a million employees across multiple facilities at numerous sites. Similar to Ron Burgundy, San Diego's beloved fictional news anchor, he's kind of a big deal. Needless to say, he's busy!

Charles regularly clocks twelve hour days with most of his time spent meeting with his team, vendors, suppliers, and senior leadership. His nights and weekends are often spent catching up on mountains of emails, monitoring key performance indicators (KPIs), reviewing a slew of reports, and catching up on the latest team news. His mantra, which he often uses in closing his emails, is "Please cascade this down to all staff." Because of Charles's demanding hours, his team is frequently tasked with similarly long hours in order to monitor his incoming emails and reports. While leadership at Charles's organization loves his directives, ideas, and plans, the front-line employees don't. They struggle to meet the demanding goals delegated from high up and feel disconnected from leadership.

So, what's the problem? Charles is working hard at sharing information and giving orders which then filter down as requested. There are charts and graphs on bulletin boards. Performance goals are consistently adjusted as the company evolves to ensure employees hit updated targets. But is his "busyness" and his directiveness pushing his people to align to the objectives, or is it pushing employees to jump off a ledge?

Charles is relying on excessive command and control when he should be relying on a team that is aligned with the mission, vision, and values. He should be building a culture where employees don't need to be in touch twelve hours a day just to stay aligned.

Starting with Self-Assessment

You want your team to align with the organization's mission, vision, and values. As is so often the case when you are a manager, the place to start is not with them but with yourself. First, you want to make sure that you yourself are creating the right conditions for alignment.

Spend some time assessing your own leadership style. Self-analysis is not always an easy task. It requires honest self-reflection (honesty is the best policy, especially in this case), courage, and a little bit of selflessness.

Begin the process of self-assessment by asking yourself questions like:

- Do I lean more toward being highly directive or non-directive as a leader?

- What do I know about my approach to communication with my team?

- What do I believe those I lead may say are my top two strengths?

- What do I believe those I lead may say are two attributes they find most frustrating?

Being direct will increase your team's clarity around goals but may undermine their commitment to those goals. If you tell someone *what* they need to accomplish that's fine, however as

Know your core company values inside and out!

soon as you begin to tell them *how* they need to accomplish it, you can run into problems. If they do it how you told them to, and it doesn't work, then they'll say it's your fault not theirs. In fact, the best place to start is not with the "what" but with the "why". If they know why something needs to be done, and specifically what they need to do, then they'll be motivated enough to figure out the how. (Check out the great TEDtalk "Start with Why" by Simon Sinek.[9])

Communication is one of the toughest things about being a manager, because no matter how good a job you think

you are doing, employees usually say there is not enough communication. When it comes to aligning their work to the organization's mission, vision and values, it's particularly important to ensure they are up to date with what the organization is focusing on and why. You will typically know about and understand the reasons for an organizational initiative, but you'll be surprised how often employees are in the dark.

32

HR Fundamentals for Non-HR Managers: Can We Be Friends? (& CYA!)

Thinking about your strengths and weaknesses helps round out the self-assessment. Note that often your weakness may be a manifestation of overused strengths. As we've noted, you want to be directive, but not too directive. You also want to be a good explainer, but not spend so much time explaining that you forget to spend time listening.

It's a good idea to talk to someone about your self-assessment. Share your reflections with a thoughtful friend or coach to get their reaction. They'll help you discover if your self-assessment is accurate and can help you figure out ways to improve.

Authentic leaders cultivate a habit of periodic self-reflection. They use honest self-assessment to adjust their own behaviors in order to lead more effectively. Michael Scott of *The Office* was once asked, "Would you rather be feared or loved?" His response, "I want people to fear how much they love me." So, this may be taking it a bit too far, but you get the idea. Managers also work collaboratively with their teams to ensure that their employees understand both team and individual goals. Effective leaders facilitate. They empower their teams to meet expectations while implementing feedback to succeed long-term. In short, the best leaders create a winning environment by fostering open, communicative, and positive team dynamics that begin with an analysis of themselves.

Make self-reflection and team facilitation a habit!

As Ron Thomas, the Managing Director of Strategy Focused Group DWC LLC, tells us in *The First Step to Great Leadership is Self-Awareness*,

> Our perception of ourselves can become severely skewed over the years...the deference shown you by your subordinates can create a false sense of who you are...Effective leaders are like..conductors...tasked with optimizing and harmonizing...efforts...to create something.. more powerful than...individual performances...The effective leader must make sure everyone understands the direction and...the journey they are on. They ensure people know what is expected of them, have the opportunity to practice their part, and receive feedback to improve individual and collective success...Effective leaders build a solid foundation...by focusing first on identifying and addressing their own development needs, and then on building relationships and fostering teamwork...[10]

What kind of leader are you, anyway?

Creating the Right Environment for Communication

Okay, you've looked inward at yourself, now look outward at the environment. What kind of environment exists in your workplace? Does it foster the kind of communication that keeps people aligned? HINT: You should never make people bow to you, sort of like what happened (we're not kidding) with Ségolène Royal, France's Ecology and Energy Minister in 2014:

> The ideal work environment is an office that doesn't feel like it's being ruled by a ruthless despot. When they walk past, you can greet them like a normal person, or maybe not at all if you're busy. But that wouldn't do for Ségolène Royal...who let her staff know that they were expected to stand whenever she passed them...She even hired a guy to walk out in front of her and announce her arrival, so employees would have enough time to leap to their feet... Isn't a forced smile pretending to be enthusiastic when we'd much rather be home in our pajamas enough? [11]

Team members may hesitate to communicate honestly in an environment where doing so creates a fear of retaliation. Remember, honesty is the best policy — except when you can lose your job! A team that is supportive of honest, diverse perspectives, with strong lateral and vertical communication is a team where members are more likely to make you aware of their concerns.

When employees mention their true concerns, then that's the real moment of truth in alignment. That's when you may learn that they don't really know what they should be doing or how they should be doing it. That's when you learn that what they are doing isn't in fact what they should be doing. That's when you learn they've run into something that seems to conflict with the organization's mission, vision or values and don't know what to do.

How you communicate is important (put your megaphone away). Too many leaders overly rely on emails and office meetings (we know this isn't you!) Remote communication can have the unintended effect of creating a "we" (management) vs. "them" (the team) environment. The wider and deeper this divide grows (thinking Grand Canyon here), the harder it can be to communicate effectively and fix problems that impact the team's alignment with the bigger picture.

Make sure the emails and meetings (which are not a bad thing) are balanced with more informal one-on-one conversations where your goal is to listen rather than talk. Strange as it may sound, getting people aligned with your goals is as much about listening to employees talk about their work as it is about you telling them what work to do.

A good tip for keeping yourself sane through your attempts to align an employee with your goals is to focus on the things that you do have control over. As Jim Clemmer tells us in his article *Stop Whining and Start Leading,*

> Focus most of your own and your team's energy on those things within your control. Pick carefully the areas or changes you would like to influence. Figure out how to let go of those things or circumstances over which you have no control. Not doing this just increases everyone's misery and creates paralysis. The poet Longfellow was right on when he observed: "have found that the best thing to do when it's raining is to let it rain." [12]

Communication and feedback should be consistent and ongoing. The choice of words matters, so think before you speak. Use inclusive, supportive language and lean towards praising positive behaviors rather than calling out people's shortcomings. Remember too that anything you put in an email or other digital form lasts forever and can easily be taken out of context. Take extra care with written communication and refrain from jokes that may be misunderstood.

How you communicate and listen sets the tone for your team.
#BigEarsSmallMouth

Communicating with Virtual Teams

There are a few special things to consider when communicating with virtual teams:

- The small social banter that builds relationships can disappear when all communication is done electronically or by video call. At the start of a meeting, make sure anyone new introduces themselves and spend a minute or two on chit chat before you get down to business.

- It's harder to know if someone isn't understanding your point on virtual teams than it is when you are face-to-face. Take more care in checking that people are clear about what they need to do and why it's worth doing. Get them to explain in their own words their understanding of what they need to do and how it fits into the bigger picture.

- It is harder to maintain focus in virtual meetings; so keep them short. Thirty minutes is good and you'll be surprised what you can accomplish in 15 minutes if you try.

Being Honest about Fear

One thing you may have a gut feeling about that you've never heard articulated, is that employees often live with a certain amount of fear. They are always afraid that you, as their manager, will make a decision that will make their lives worse. You almost certainly have good intentions, yet that doesn't mean employees won't be hypersensitive to real or perceived slights.

There's a model David Rock developed he calls "putting on the SCARF." The SCARF Model (Status, Certainty, Autonomy, Relatedness, and Fairness) encourages you to remain aware of the things employees may be afraid of. In a nutshell, the SCARF model says:

- Be careful that what you say doesn't threaten someone's **status** (e.g. make them feel or look unimportant).

Status + Certainty + Autonomy + Relatedness + Fairness

- Be careful to enhance **certainty**. You can't avoid uncertainty entirely, but it causes stress in employees, so always check to see if employees have a clear grasp of what is expected or what will happen.

- Be careful about taking away **autonomy**. Employees don't like it when they have no control, as often as possible give them a choice about how they approach their work.

- Pay attention to **relatedness**, which refers to whether an employee sees another individual as a friend or a stranger. Employees need the comfort of feeling they are working with people they know.

- Finally comes **fairness**, or rather the perception of fairness. Employees can be terribly sensitive to any hint of unfairness so you need to be too.

As David Rock notes in *Managing with the Brain Mind*,

...The SCARF model provides...conscious awareness... [of] potentially fraught interactions. It helps alert you to people's core concerns...and shows you how to calibrate your words and actions to better effect. Start by reducing the threats inherent in...leaders' behavior...Threat always trumps reward because the threat response is strong... Skilled leaders understand this and act accordingly. [13]

= SCARF

Thinking about Total Rewards

If you are truly committed to having your team aligned with the corporate mission, vision, and values, eventually you'll need to confront the issue of total rewards (i.e. base pay, bonuses, benefits, opportunities to learn, work-life balance, opportunities to get ahead, etc.).

The main thing to watch for are any aspects of total rewards that run in direct opposition to the goals you are preaching. For example, if the mission includes providing great value to the customer, but employees are rewarded for selling services the customer doesn't need, then it becomes impossible for them to take the company's mission seriously.

Similarly, if the company's values include taking good care of employees, but the benefits offered are terrible then again, it's hard for employees to believe the values are anything more than window dressing.

There will be limits on how much influence you have to change total reward policies. Your role is to raise the issue with more senior managers and help them understand how unaligned reward policies are undermining the company's investment in getting employees focused on the right things.

One thing you can do that doesn't have many limits, is to continue to reward employees with praise when they live up to the mission, vision, and values. As Ron Thomas tells us in *The Two Most Powerful Leadership Phrases*,

> A person who feels appreciated will always do more than expected...The two most powerful phrases of any leader are: "Thank you", "I appreciate you"....[14]

Your team will "feel the love" with a thoughtful approach to compensation planning!

38

HR Fundamentals for Non-HR Managers: Can We Be Friends? (& CYA!)

Another thing you can do is help employees understand how rewards decisions are made at your company. In *It's the Manager,* Clifton and Harter note:

> While pay is a personal matter, criteria for pay increases and promotions should be transparent...Be clear with employees about how their pay compares with what they could get somewhere else...be especially clear about the criteria for making more money in a given job...the desire for fairness and equity is a basic human need...be prepared to describe how you measure performance...[15]

It's All about Change

You may be thinking that you will have to manage people through these changes. There's a technical term for that:

"change management". (At last a buzzword that makes sense!) Check out the ADKAR Change Model, founded by entrepreneur and author Jeff Hiatt. The model shows the change process in five steps:

- Awareness: Communicate pending changes

- Desire: Inspire support for changes

- Knowledge: Gather info about changes

- Ability: Encourage flexible changes

- Reinforcement: Reinforce the changes

Whenever you want to introduce change, refer to this model to ensure you don't miss any key steps.

ADKAR Change Model

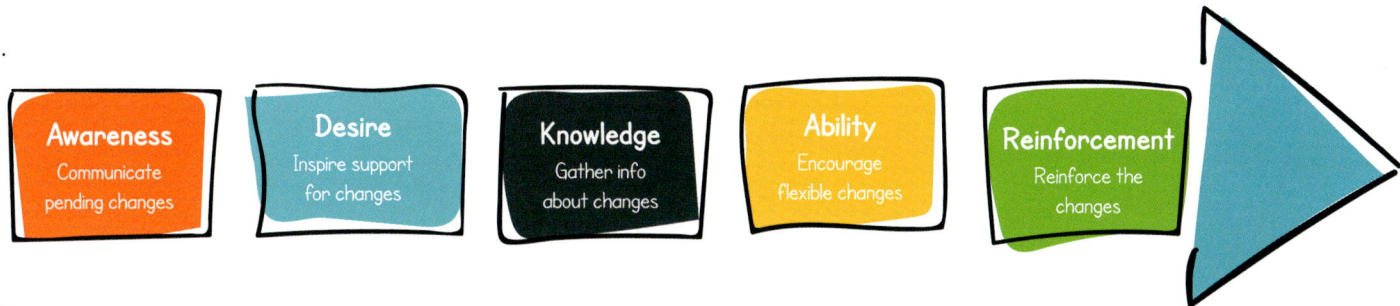

Awareness
Communicate pending changes

Desire
Inspire support for changes

Knowledge
Gather info about changes

Ability
Encourage flexible changes

Reinforcement
Reinforce the changes

Know your company's goals and your team's alignment.

What is working and what is not?

Back to the Story

Let's think back to our story about Charles, the hyper-busy manager always telling people exactly what they need to do. Charles needs to step back and take a more comprehensive approach to leadership. That will start with a frank self-assessment (likely supported with some wise comments from a friend or coach) so that he can see the limitations of the existing approach.

He can start thinking of the environment he needs to create to get the results he wants, and how his communication style can support that. It's easy for managers to slip into a sub-optimal style, with a little training they can redirect their approach and become more effective.

He was so focused on the tasks that he overlooked the fact that this style was not effective in getting the best out of his team.

Summing Up

Your role as a manager is critical because you lead the most precious resources any organization has (which is the company bank account, right? Just kidding!).

40

HR Fundamentals for Non-HR Managers: Can We Be Friends? (& CYA!)

Obviously, we're referring to your people. As such, a significant amount of your time as a manager must be dedicated to properly developing, guiding, and coaching the people on your team so that they stay aligned with the company's mission, vision, and values.

Alignment comes from getting several different factors right and it won't happen all at once. Here are some things to reflect on as we end the chapter:

- How do I communicate with my team?

- How do I coach them?

- What are the weaknesses of my current approach? Strengths?

- How should I modify my approach?

Approach alignment with optimism (yes, that's right — the glass is ALWAYS half full). You can do it and so can your team.

Let's take a few minutes to do a quick practice activity on strategic alignment.

Effective leaders show rather than tell.
#WalkTheTalk

Get Out Your Trowel and Cement: Strategic Brick Laying Activity

In thinking about the company and team objectives, how are you lining up? How is your team lining up? Take a moment to jot down the goals in the first box. Then, highlight the ways you and your team are achieving those goals, leveraging the company values. In the second box, write down the areas that need improvement. Review these with your team to strategize on ways to remedy the issues.

Goals and How We Are Achieving Them

My Observations to Areas that Need Improvement

SECTION 2

Creating a respectful environment:
Improving Diversity, Equity,
and Inclusion

EMBRACING DIVERSITY

BE THE MANAGER WHO IS SCRUPULOUSLY FAIR

Key Terms and Definitions

Diversity – Understanding that each individual is unique and embracing those differences (such as different cultures, gender, personality)

Inclusion – Ensuring people feel a valued part of the team.

Equity – Equal opportunity and fair treatment for all.

The Issue

Creating a respectful work environment hinges on knowing the differences between diversity, equity, and inclusion. A respectful environment will help create good team dynamics, while also staying in compliance with legislation and the company's policies.

A Short Story

Patrick, an African American gentleman, was interviewing for an executive role for a well-known brand in New York. He was meeting with the President of the company, Laura, a Caucasian American woman. Laura had her back turned as Patrick entered her office. As he came in, she turned around and stared at Patrick. Her jaw dropped like she was about to catch a fly! The surprised look on her face said it all. Laura had made assumptions based on her previous conversations with him that he was of a different ethnicity, and not African American.

Clearly flustered, she never fully regained her composure. Sensing her discomfort, Patrick knew it was unlikely he'd be offered the job, and he probably wouldn't want it even if it was offered. The meeting lasted just twenty minutes. It was the shortest interview at that level that Patrick had ever had. He checked their website later and saw that her company talked about how they embrace diversity—this almost made him laugh. It was another case where an organization espoused diversity without having learned how to create an inclusive environment.

44

HR Fundamentals for Non-HR Managers: Can We Be Friends? (& CYA!)

A few months passed. Patrick received a call from a recruiter for a leadership position in another division of Laura's company. He immediately responded, "Sorry, but I'm not interested." He knew there were other companies that had figured out how to be inclusive, he'd wait for an opportunity to work for one of them.

Why care about Diversity, Equity, and Inclusion

Diversity, equity, and inclusion matter because they are the path to getting and keeping the best talent. They're also the path to having a productive work environment where everyone can contribute, and where conflict is minimized. If you want the most effective team, you need to ask yourself:

Partner with HR (and CYA)

HR needs you to be proactive in creating an inclusive culture.

- Are we hiring the best talent or are we swayed by factors (like gender, ethnicity, attractiveness) that are not related to performance?

- Have we created an equitable environment that will retain and motivate everyone on the team?

- Am I doing what I need to do as a manager to embrace diversity, equity, and inclusion?

Defining Diversity

How does diversity translate to the real world? The University of Oregon offers a robust definition of diversity:

> ... The concept of diversity encompasses acceptance and respect. It means understanding that each individual is unique, and recognizing our...differences. These can be along the dimensions of race, ethnicity, gender, sexual orientation, socio-economic status, age, physical abilities, religious beliefs, political beliefs, or other ideologies...moving beyond simple tolerance to embracing and... Celebrating...diversity...[16]

Let's unbundle this a little:

- Diversity exists upon many different dimensions, not just gender and ethnic origin.

- The goal isn't simply to tolerate difference; it's to embrace it to achieve business success.

Though the concept is somewhat fluid, let's define diversity as understanding, accepting, and respecting people with different identifiers such as:

- race,
- color,
- ethnicity,
- national origin,
- ancestry,
- genetic information,
- age,
- physical ability,

- pregnancy and related stages,
- mental ability,
- socio-economic status,
- gender diversity or sexual orientation and gender identity,
- military and veteran status,
- arrest record, incarceration history, caregiver status,

- marital/family status,
- religious beliefs,
- physical appearance including weight,
- creed,
- political values, and/or
- any other characteristic protected by federal, state or local laws.

Humans are diverse in many interesting ways
#UniquePeople

Compliance Don'ts

- Don't make any comments about racial or gender traits, even in jest.

- Don't be dismissive towards employee concerns about diversity.

- Don't turn a blind eye to employees who violate HR's diversity policies.

Think for a moment about all the diversity that exists on your team. If you are aware of and embrace those differences, you'll get better performance.

Think for a moment about all the diversity that exists in the world. If you are screening out potential hires on the identifiers such as those listed on the previous page, then you are missing out on the best talent, which may come in many diverse and different forms.

Defining Inclusion

If diversity is about differences between people, then inclusion refers to something we all have in common: we all want to feel like we belong. Hence, we can keep our definition quite simple. In everyday manager's terms, "inclusion is making sure each employee feels included."

Limeade's article, *Inclusion in Your Workplace,* tells us that:

> The key to inclusion is making sure each employee feels included...You need true commitment from everyone, every day and throughout an organization, to create a culture that feels inclusive. Leaders also need to show they authentically value the people behind the ideas and experiences. [17]

Think for a moment:

- Do I know my team well enough that I understand what's unique about them and any concerns they might have?

- Do we ever do things that will exclude people? (e.g. team pub nights that exclude people who don't drink.)

- Do I make sufficient efforts to respond to individual needs? (e.g. time off for religious holidays, etc.)

- Do I or my team make assumptions about an individual based on gender or ethnic origin, instead of finding out what that individual is like?

- Do I show authentic respect and appreciation for each team member?

- Do I make a special effort to include team members who don't seem to be fitting in?

Don't let subtle biases undermine giving equal opportunity to all.

It's all pretty straightforward in theory. In practice, you'll have to work hard to overcome stereotypes, lack of awareness of differences, and the human tendency to break up into "in-groups" and "out-groups." (This means don't turn back to high school times when the "cool kids" snubbed the "uncool kids.") Pay attention, work at improving inclusion, and you will see results.

Defining Equity

So, we have taken a look at diversity and inclusion. Now, let's take a look at equity. Chron Writer and Editor Sophie Johnson notes in *The Advantages of Equity in the Workplace*,

> Equity in a workplace means everyone receives fair treatment. There's a transparency... and everyone knows what to expect in terms of consequences and rewards. When equity exists, people have equal access to opportunities. It sets up an advantageous environment for both the employees and the employer. [18]

Equity, simply put, means "equal opportunity for all." How do you do this? Engage people on your team, particularly those who feel marginalized, by providing fair opportunities to grow, contribute, and develop. Keep this equal, across the team, and your practice becomes your culture. Equal = equal!

Think for a moment:

- Do all of my team members feel this workplace is fair? If they don't, why do they think that?

- Do members on my team believe that there is an equal opportunity for advancement?

- Might we need to increase transparency of how decisions are made around pay, promotion, and how tasks are assigned, so they understand it is fair?

- Or might they be right that it isn't really fair?

Your team will care a lot about equity, and they may have a different lens on it than you do. Take the time to see how people feel. (Look we know that you are not intentionally being unfair, but let's be real, employees may see things differently. You gotta figure that out.)

Inclusion in a Time of Virtual Work

Hey, now that you are getting a good handle on diversity, equity, and inclusion you'll be glad to hear those concepts all apply to virtual work. Is there anything special you should look out for? Sure there is. For example, Jeff Bezos will have no trouble finding a quiet home office in one of his mansions — your team may not live in large mansions, so be sensitive to challenges they may face.

Don't let out of sight be out of mind. Reach out to your employees who are working remotely.

Another thing to consider is that people who have English as a second language might have a harder time understanding the conversation in conference calls than they would face to face. It's just a matter of recognizing different people are in different situations, being sensitive to that, and dealing with concerns as they arise.

Dealing with Concerns Brought to You

As a manager, you will be working to embrace diversity, ensure equity, and enhance inclusion. That's the easy part. The tough part is when an employee comes to you, saying there is a problem. This is really where the rubber hits the road. You must not shrug it off as just one more employee complaint. Listen carefully, think before you speak, and act.

Here are some things to keep in mind:

- Start with a sense of compassion; if a team member is upset about something you need to understand where they are coming from and what they are facing if you want to find a way to help.

- Remember, your perspective may be — and likely is — very different than the individual perspectives of your team members. Put aside your own perspective and work hard to see the world through their eyes.

- Word choices or actions that may be perceived as "harmless" by you may be perceived differently or even offensively by members of your team. Be sure to address concerns immediately.

- Don't hesitate to contact HR for guidance. They can provide tips before you sit down with the individual to learn more about their concern. They can tell you about policies and legislation. They may even be able to help facilitate a meeting if the situation is particularly sensitive.

- Use your company's protocol to determine if the words or actions in question are discriminatory in any way and follow HR's guidance for the next steps. Not only is this the best way to prevent a lawsuit, but it's the right thing to do!

A key to being successful in managing diversity, equity, and inclusion is taking concerns seriously and handling them carefully. If you need help doing this, don't be afraid to ask

Partner with HR

Make sure the diversity of your team is trending in the right direction

a mentor or HR. This is a valuable way to partner with your HR team members. (Yes, believe it or not, HR is a great free resource when you learn how to work with them.)

Using A Strengths-Based Approach to Improve Diversity and Inclusion

Okay, talking about employees' concerns felt tough didn't it? Let's look at something that has a happier feel. You can use a strengths-based approach to improve diversity and inclusion.

Clifton and Harter point us to the value of a strengths-based approach in *It's the Manager*. They note,

> The best strategy to improve inclusion across your organization is to adopt a strengths-based approach to employee development and to build a strengths-based culture...Not only does a strengths-based approach give people a shortcut for getting to know one another and creating positive ongoing dialogue, but organizations with strengths-based cultures consistently outperform their competitors. [19]

50

HR Fundamentals for Non-HR Managers: Can We Be Friends? (& CYA!)

What does this have to do with diversity and inclusion? It means we are seeing past any surface identifiers like gender, race, or religion and embracing what's great about each unique individual. Nothing makes people feel more valued and included than when you recognize and leverage their strengths.

As a manager, it's your job to find the strengths of your team members so you can help position them to leverage those strengths. You will be creating a more high functioning team as you capitalize on the strengths of each person.

"Mirror, mirror, on the wall…" Who doesn't want to be able to focus on their strengths and see themselves as thriving?

What is a strengths-based approach? It's an approach of focusing on what people are good at and leveraging that. It stands in contrast to a weakness-based approach where you focus on what's wrong with people and try to fix it.

Imagine you have an employee who is not detail-oriented. You could coach them, criticize them, train them, and yell at them, all in an attempt to fix the problem. OR you could give them a job that matches their strengths (which might be customer service).

> Included employees are engaged employees

What We Can Learn from the Limeade Institute

The Limeade Institute conducted a study in which they surveyed over 2,000 US employees about their feelings regarding inclusion in the workplace.

The study focused on how inclusion was perceived by US employees vs. how it was actually implemented between teams, their management, and company leadership. Limeade found that friendships between colleagues or peers on a team can help create feelings of inclusion, closely followed by vertical connections between management and team members. The study also showed that employees who work in inclusive environments are:

- 28% more engaged at work,
- 43% more committed to their company,
- 19% more satisfied with their lives and well-being, and
- 51% more likely to recommend their employer or organization. [20]

Wow! And what manager would not want to have their team members feeling included, engaged, happy, and productive? You got this! Go, coach, go!

Staying Compliant with the Law and Company Policies

There are many laws and policies related to diversity, equity, and inclusion. Keep up to date by taking courses on:

- Unconscious Bias Training
- Diversity Training
- Discrimination Training
- Affirmative Action Training
- ADA Training
- Conflict Resolution Training

Back to the Story

The President in the story probably never received effective training in diversity, equity, and inclusion. This lack of skill in handling diversity is hurting her company now because she can't get the best talent.

Patrick luckily will be fine. There are enough companies that have embraced diversity not just in word but also in deed that he'll find a place that sees his strengths.

Summing Up

Diversity reflects the fact that there are many kinds of individual differences, and that we should embrace those differences rather than fall prey to bias or stereotypes.

Inclusion encourages managers to ensure that everyone on a diverse team feels like they belong. And finally, equity reminds us to put a special emphasis on being fair.

As the manager:

- When you take the lead at being inclusive, it will help set the tone for what is acceptable and expected on your team.
- When you discover areas of deficiency, rally the team for their input to help put actionable measures in place to create change.
- When you clearly communicate expectations, it will go a long way to build a culture of respect and inclusion that will help diversity flourish!

As the manager, you need to take the lead on inclusion

A huge return awaits you in the investment of diversity and inclusion in your team. Engaged teams, retention and increased productivity and profitability are just some of the results you can anticipate.

Even as you do your best to create an inclusive, equitable environment there are bound to be employees who raise concerns. This is a real moment of truth for you. You need to take these concerns seriously and handle them with skill.

Now let's work through a quick activity to apply these ideas to your own unique situation.

Build A Better Bond: A Diversity, Equity, and Inclusion Activity

Current State Box
Manager Perspective

Think briefly about your team. Is it diverse? What makes it diverse? Could your team be more diverse? How? Does your team nurture inclusivity? How about equity? Note your responses and thoughts about the current state of diversity, equity, and inclusion on your team in this box.

Current State Box
Diverse Perspective

Now take a moment to think about how your responses would change if you were of a different age, race, gender identity, sexual orientation, religion, physical appearance, or ability. Would you feel the same way? Or would your perspectives change? Capture these new thoughts in this box. Collect diverse feedback to consider as you fill in your alternate perspectives below.

Better Bond Box
Optimized Perspective

Identify and write the steps you can take to improve diversity, equity, and inclusion on your team based on team feedback and your own thought processes in this box. Implement some of your ideas and return to update this box as diversity, equity, and inclusion evolve on your team.

EMBRACING INCLUSION

BE THE MANAGER WHO CREATES A WELCOMING CULTURE

Key Terms and Definitions

Cultural competence – **The ability to understand, communicate with and effectively interact with people across cultures.**

Cultural proficiency – **The ability to identify and challenge one's own cultural assumptions, values and beliefs, and to make a commitment to communicating at the cultural interface**

The Issue

There are many different types of people in the world. We don't always get along well. As a manager, you can improve teamwork and retention by creating an inclusive environment. Let's look at how you do that.

A Short Story

Michael is a transgender employee who has been employed at the Oceania Kayak Corporation for the past six years. Following his transition from female to male, he stated to his manager that he would like to be addressed with the pronouns: he, him, and his. He also noted that he wants to use the men's restroom and be called Michael instead of his given name of Michelle. The manager has had numerous other "issues" on his team to deal with, so he decided to continue to call him by his legal first name, Michelle, rather than by his preferred name. Michael considers this behavior workplace harassment since his manager and colleagues are not using the proper pronouns or name, as requested. The manager feels that this is an unreasonable request, and responds that even though other team members are often referred to by nicknames (rather than their full, proper, legal names) she will still unilaterally refer to Michael as Michelle only, which is his legal first name. The manager has other things on her mind and doesn't see using Michael's old name as a problem.

Get to know each individual and show sensitivity in finding ways to include them.

- *being aware of one's own world view*
- *developing positive attitudes towards cultural differences*
- *gaining knowledge of different cultural practices and world views*
- *developing skills for communication and interaction across cultures*

Cultural proficiency "requires more than becoming culturally aware or practicing tolerance". Rather, it is the ability to "identify and challenge one's own cultural assumptions, values and beliefs, and to make a commitment to communicating at the cultural interface". [21]

So, it isn't a quick game of "Go Fish." It is more like a month-long game of chess. The baseline for cultural proficiency? Respect. But notice it goes beyond everyday respect. Being culturally proficient moves into the more difficult world of challenging your own assumptions.

The difficulty for the manager is that just because she believes there isn't a problem, doesn't mean there isn't one. This will come back to bite her if she doesn't learn how to manage a diverse team.

Develop Your Cultural Competency

Managing your diverse team should be a cinch, right? Famous last words! You cannot truly build an inclusive team by simply throwing people together and then wrapping standards and expectations around them like they are holiday gifts in a basket wrapped in cellophane! In order to thrive as a collaborative team, let's take a look at what, exactly, the terms "culturally competent" and "culturally proficient"mean.

An Australian group, ACECQA, puts it nicely,

> Cultural competence is the ability to understand, communicate with and effectively interact with people across cultures. Cultural competence encompasses:

56

HR Fundamentals for Non-HR Managers: Can We Be Friends? (& CYA!)

In our story, the manager felt she was treating the transgender employee with enough respect. Where the manager fell short was in challenging her own assumptions about what was required. What the manager felt was important in terms of showing respect didn't align with the employee's view. It's not that employees are always right, but in matters of inclusion, their views always need to be considered seriously. (Yes, this is true even if you are busy.)

It is likely that no one warned you about the need for cultural proficiency. All the other things you learned about being a manager (ie. setting goals, communicating, managing processes, and so on) were just additions to your knowledge base. Cultural proficiency is asking you to *challenge* your worldview. It's asking you to go from "I'm confident this is correct" to, "Hmmm, if I see this from a new and unfamiliar perspective, I may not be correct."

Partner with HR (and CYA)

The main thing HR asks of you is to show sensitivity towards each unique individual.

It is tough, but now that you have an awareness of the need for an enhanced understanding of your own and others' worldviews, you are off to a good start.

Do a Personal Self-Assessment

Let's start with your personal situation. Take a second to perform a quick, personal inventory and assess the cross-cultural climate you currently live and work in:

- How many people in your personal circle of friends come from different cultures?

- Are you close with people from backgrounds different than your own?

- Can you think of cultures that you don't interact with at all?

Most people have some diversity in their social life while remaining unconnected to certain groups. It's those areas where we don't have connections or understanding that should concern us. That's where our blind spots are.

What blind spots might you have? To make this more concrete, think about the people on your team. Are there people whose ethnic background, gender preferences, or life story are very different from your own? Those are the people you'll want to pay close attention to as you develop your cultural proficiency.

Can you think of anything they do that seems odd to you? Do you recall any situations where their sense of what to do was different from what you felt was the right action? These situations provide clues to possible cultural differences. As a manager you need to be aware of those differences if you want a productive team. Once you have that awareness, you can take any necessary actions to create a feeling of inclusion.

Helping Your Team with Cultural Proficiency

One of the challenges you face is that inclusiveness isn't just a result of how you treat your team; it comes from how they treat each other. Once you have improved your own cultural proficiency, how do you bring that to your team?

A good way to start is by having discussions, both one on one and in small groups, about diversity with your team. Find out what it means to each team member to be respected and included. Find out if there are things about other employees that make them uncomfortable. You don't want to make a big deal about this, you just want to make it possible for people to raise concerns so that you are in a position to provide guidance.

When your team members talk to each other about their own personal situation, it can enhance familiarity, comfort, and empathy for and with one another.

This isn't high school so no jocks vs nerds battles. Everyone is on the same team.

It is also helpful to provide cultural competency training and workshops on inclusion. The goal is to bridge any cultural divide and help to create an inclusive environment. You may not be sitting around a campfire, singing camp songs and roasting marshmallows for s'mores, but the warmth of unity enhances a work environment like no other! Training is something your HR department can help you deliver. Don't just slide a note under their door asking for training and walk away. Talk to them about what you want to achieve; see what they suggest and collaborate.

You can also take the lead by being a good role model in acting inclusively. Beyond that, watch for offensive or discriminatory behaviors, which may be implicitly accepted. For example, laughing off offensive comments or jokes with the unspoken understanding that "everyone knows it's wrong but thinks it's funny" (blonde jokes, anyone?) can lead to exclusion and/or discrimination against those team members who may be genuinely offended. Make it clear that you won't tolerate that offensive behavior and explain why.

The Landmine of Unfairness

Enough of the happy talk about helping your team become culturally proficient. Let's talk about something difficult. One of the big problems you may face is when someone feels they have been treated unfairly, and that lack of fairness is related to a diversity issue. It's bad enough if someone says you haven't been fair in how you assign tasks; it gets even worse when they imply it's due to bias.

Remember even the perception of unfairness is a problem you have to deal with. Acting fairly isn't enough. You have to be seen to act fairly or all hell can break loose. Let's check out what Dr. David Rock has to say,

> The perception that an event has been unfair generates a strong response...stirring hostility and undermining trust.....[22]

Whoa! You don't want to go there. Take a moment to think about something in your own life that made you feel that you had been treated unfairly. Perhaps you felt an unfair conclusion had been drawn about you, or an unfair decision had been made that impacted you:

- How did you feel about it then?
- How do you feel about it now, as you remember it?

If you can avoid putting anyone on your team in a situation where they feel this way, then you're on the right path.

> **Employees are deeply attuned to unfairness. Be transparent in how you make decisions.**

> **Build a sense of inclusion by taking the time to show each employee that you notice and appreciate their accomplishments.**

Here is the thing about unfairness in a diverse environment. You may be unfair without realizing it. Furthermore, your idea of what's fair may be different from what your diverse team thinks is fair. Recognize that members of your team will likely have different perspectives than yours (this doesn't mean they're wrong, like your overly opinionated Aunt Edith). Instead, you should seek ways to incorporate their ideas. Accept constructive feedback without thinking of it as an attack on your personal values or beliefs. And, don't be a jerk about it!

How to be Seen as Being Fair

The key tactic for being seen as being fair is clarity and transparency. Be clear about what you expect from people. Make sure the processes by which they are assessed are transparent. (Transparency simply means that the processes and facts behind a decision are communicated.)

Maybe exactly what you expect of other people isn't something you've nailed down in your own mind. It's time to do so. If you have clarity and you communicate it, then you're less likely to be accused of being unfair.

Also, do some self-monitoring. Are you hypercritical of some people? Do you let other people off the hook too easily? Are you word choices and tone consistent across the team? Remember no "teacher's pets!"

A Step You Can Take to Make Inclusiveness Easier

Let's move from something hard to something easy: appreciation. Building a culturally competent and inclusive team environment can enhance the effectiveness and happiness of your entire team. You can make great strides in building the right environment simply by taking a minute here and a minute there to show appreciation.

Don't worry, be happy! Author and Instructional Designer Corrinne King supports this approach in her article, *How to Manage a Diverse Team*, as she states,

> Employees who feel appreciated are more likely to contribute more and care about a company's success....make sure that each person is participating equally on the team...[23]

Love the simplicity of this concept. Make sure everyone believes they are appreciated beyond a shadow of a doubt and that no one feels they are just biding time on the bench. The team that plays well together will stay together!

> **Don't be the scary manager that employees are afraid to speak to.**

You are bound to make mistakes in trying to be inclusive. There are bound to be times when some employees feel a decision is not fair. If you create a positive environment by showing appreciation, then your team is far less likely to take offense. The transgender employee who genuinely knows their work is valued will be better able to respond to, and talk to you, about any missteps you make.

Next up is another staple of effective management: communication. We couldn't be more clear about clear communication when looking at various facets of team management! Culturally competent management of your team also means seeking to avoid misunderstandings by:

- creating open communication channels to empower team members to voice thoughts/opinions without fear of repercussion,
- conducting in-person conversations, when possible, to avoid any risk of misunderstanding, and
- using an honest and transparent approach.

Be approachable (no, please don't use a perma-grin; that's just creepy!), so that your team feels comfortable having difficult conversations with you or asking for help. Intervene quickly if any tension is sensed or communicated (anger meter headed toward tilt), and make sure no one feels bullied or ignored by you or other team members. Remember, conflicts will most certainly arise, and when they do, it is better to address them sooner than later. You don't want to be the Captain shouting, "Man the lifeboats! The ship is sinking!"

Foster clearer communications by seeking to understand before being understood. OK, that sounds a little philosophical (where's Socrates when you need him?) , but the chances are quite good that the person who is perpetrating the offensive behavior may be unaware of the nature of the offense. In these cases, seek to:

- understand,
- inform,
- educate, and
- coach.

This approach will go a long way toward fostering clearer communication and better collaboration and a feeling of inclusiveness.

Take a moment to reflect on some of the key points we've been covering:

- Showing respect for individuals
- Taking the time to talk to them about their individual (diverse) situation
- Showing appreciation for their contributions
- Opening up good lines of communication

- Do make sure that everyone can feel included in team events. This means being aware of barriers for people with disabilities, dietary restrictions, and religious issues. Basically you need to make sure everyone can join in.

"When people come to work, they bring their age, gender, culture, faith, family, finances, past experiences, and dreams. In whole-person hiring, you welcome this data, explore the advantages, and find ways to leverage these life experiences." [24]

Increased diversity can lead to better business results.

Back to the Story

Michael's manager probably has never known a transgender person before. Because the manager lacked understanding of Michael's perspective she failed to take some simple steps that would have made the employee feel included. If the manager were more culturally competent, she would have taken Michael's concerns more seriously, and found a way to address them.

Do you see an underlying theme here? Being a culturally competent manager is grounded in being a good manager; a manager who is attuned to each team member.

Is There a Counter Argument Against Diversity?

We've been talking about how to promote diversity; is there a counterargument against it?

One of the common arguments against special measures to increase diversity in the workplace is that a company just wants to hire the best people, regardless of their gender, color, cultural background, age, or personal beliefs. Sound fair? It misses one crucial point: someone's background is a quality in and of itself. Who you are is just as important to employers as your experiences and skill sets. Dan Medlin of ProActive Talent states,

62

HR Fundamentals for Non-HR Managers: Can We Be Friends? (& CYA!)

> **Increased diversity can lead to better business results.**

Hopefully, someone in HR or even the manager's manager, would take some time to help the manager see the situation more clearly. Of course, HR may not even know this problem is occuring. That's why you as a manager should ask HR for help if you, or someone on your team, are uncertain about how to handle a situation.

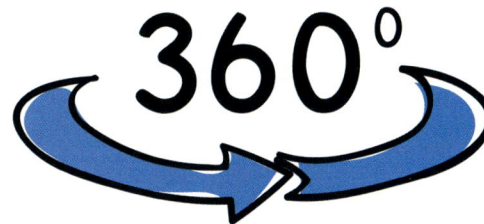

Summing Up

Cultural competence is an ability to understand, communicate with, and effectively interact with people across cultures. Cultural proficiency involves the ability to question your own mindset as a step towards better understanding others.

To improve you and your team's cultural competency and proficiency:

- Start with some self-assessment; you may have gaps in your cultural awareness that need to be filled.

- Help your team become better at inclusiveness by collaborating with HR to provide meaningful cultural competency training and workshops on inclusion.

- Be especially alert to real or perceived unfairness and provide clarity about expectations. Transparency about how decisions are made will also help.

- Make your life easier by showing appreciation and having good communication. Be approachable so that your team feels comfortable having difficult conversations and asking for help.

That's a lot to take in! It's time for a quick practice activity on cultural competency.

360^0

Throw Out the Broken Bricks: A Cultural Competency Activity

The following activity will help you and your team identify any hidden biases or stereotypes that may interfere with being culturally competent. Conduct this activity with your team, during a lunch and learn or other group learning period or activity that you have scheduled. Allow thirty minutes to an hour for this activity. Start by revealing (in handouts or on a PPT) the Fact/Opinion chart below. You may add or substitute with statements of your own. Evaluate the "Fact" and "Opinion" columns with your team. Which statements are actually facts and which appear to be opinions to you? To your team? Are the statements in the right columns?

Point out that stereotypes and biases are often based on opinions that are thought of as facts. Divide your team into pairs or small groups. In the space provided, have each group or pair label each statement as either fact or opinion. When they are done, take time to discuss.

Were the statements labeled as facts truly based on fact? What evidence supports the conclusions drawn? For each statement listed as a fact that has little or no factual support

or evidence, list some of the additional information you may need in order to determine if the statement is a fact or an opinion.

Then discuss whether the opinions listed show bias or not. If they do, what makes them biased? Is there any factual information or evidence that disproves the biased or opinion-based statements?

Allow every team member the opportunity to contribute meaningfully to the discussion and share your own perspectives and opinions as well, being sure to set the tone for an inclusive, non-discriminatory, discussion that is culturally respectful and sensitive. As the manager, you may want to share your thoughts and perspectives after everyone else. This may encourage your team to share, without knowing if their ideas differ from yours.

Statement	Is this Statement Fact or an Opinion?	Need Info	Shows Bias
Men are more logical than women			
Most people on earth are not native English speakers			
People with accents are often uneducated or unintelligent			
Sexual preference has no bearing on work ability			
Most minorities live in or come from low-income areas			
Many immigrants to the US are well-educated			
Most Asians are proficient in math, science, and technology			
Physical ability should not impact hiring decisions			
Most Americans are racist			
Africans are less qualified than American-born citizens			
Multilingualism requires a high level of intelligence			
Women should be compensated more than men			
Technology can be used by all employees equally			
Muslims can pose a terrorism risk in the workplace			
Minority employees are prone to steal from the company			
Only American-born citizens should lead in American companies			
Compensation should be based on qualifications			

Hook, Line, and Sinker:
Catching the best talent

EMPLOYMENT BRANDING

ISN'T THAT THE JOB OF THE MARKETING DEPARTMENT?

Key Terms and Definitions

Employment brand – **How the people you would like to hire feel about your organization.**

Employment Value Proposition (EVP) – **The specifics like pay, benefits, and opportunities to advance your career that attract and retain employees.**

The Issue

The first step in attracting good employees is creating an organization where people want to work. Communicating why your company is a great place to work is called "Employer Branding" and the result is an "Employment Brand."

If your organization isn't a desirable place to work, then a realistic look at the employment brand will point you towards what you need to fix.

As a manager involved in recruiting for your team, you should understand what this brand is and your role in using it to attract great people.

A Short Story

A woman was tragically killed by a bus and her soul arrived at the Pearly Gates. She was welcomed by The GateKeeper who said, "Welcome and you're in luck you have two job offers, one in heaven and one in hell."

"Job offers?" said the woman. "Well, I didn't know that's how it worked, but I can tell you right now I want the one in heaven."

"Well," said The GateKeeper. "We need to follow the HR process and that means taking a tour of the operations in Heaven and a day in Hell, and then you choose where you'd like to go for all eternity."

Since they were already "upstairs" she took the tour of heaven first where her job would be to drive a limo taking angels to various sites in Heaven. It was all very nice, much as you would expect. She was ready to take the job, but The GateKeeper insisted that she tour the other place as well and consider their offer. He led her to an elevator, and she pressed "Down."

When she arrived at Hell she was surprised how beautiful it was. There were foosball tables and a cafeteria with free gourmet food. Her job was to drive a limo taking devils to various sites in Hell, but the Devil told her that it was a flex-time job and she only had to work as many hours as she liked.

Everyone in the main office laughed and smiled, and the Devil seemed to be the most thoughtful and generous boss she'd ever met. As a bonus, many of her friends, including quite a number of ex-boyfriends, were already in Hell and they assured her it was a wonderful place.

Later, when she returned to The GateKeeper she said that while Heaven made a good offer, the one from Hell was even better and she couldn't turn it down.

Accordingly, The GateKeeper took her to the elevator and she went back down to Hell. When she arrived she was led to a smelly office crammed with miserable looking co-workers. The Devil yelled at her to get started on her 48 hour driving shift. "What about flex-time?" she asked. "Nope, that policy is no longer in force."

After two horrific days, she confronted the Devil. "How is it that everything was so wonderful on the tour and is so terrible now?"

"Oh that's simple," he explained. "We always make a big effort to impress candidates, but if you wanted to know the real employment brand you should have checked out Glassdoor."

Yesterday we were recruiting you. Today, you're staff!!

Section 3 • Chapter 1 • Employment Branding: Isn't that the job of the Marketing Department?

69

> **Job seekers know better than ever what it's really like to work in your company.**
>
> **There's no place to hide!**

Let's Not Be Like the Devil

One lesson you can take from the story is that an employment brand—the image an organization presents—plays a powerful role in attracting staff. The lesson you don't want to follow is the idea that the employment brand should be fake. A fake employment brand will alienate people and lead to high levels of turnover. Furthermore, it's getting harder and harder to fake the employment brand when job seekers can check out sites like Glassdoor.

If your work environment isn't pleasant, don't try to dress it up with fancy marketing. Fix it, and then you'll have an honest employment brand that will attract the right people.

Learning the Lingo

Your employment brand is how *the people you would like to hire* feel about your organization. If you are an advertising firm, then you hope that the most talented people in the advertising industry believe you are a desirable place to work. If you are a hard-driving, no-nonsense, sales-focused company, you hope sales reps know that so that the non-hard-driving people won't apply and the hard-driving ones will. If you run an automotive repair shop in Kalamazoo, you hope mechanics in the community think it's a great shop.

"An EVP defines the essence of your company — how it is unique and what it stands for." [20]

There is a related term called the Employment Value Proposition (EVP). Whereas brand is about the overall image, the EVP focuses on specifics like pay, benefits, and opportunities to advance your career. The brand is what gets candidates to apply for your jobs; the EVP is how you close the deal.

So, What is the Employment Brand of your Organization?

It's useful to know what people, in particular the people you would like to hire, think of your company. If you keep asking the recruiting team to get you Batman and instead the candidates are more like SpongeBob Squarepants, then maybe there is a problem with the employment brand.

70

HR Fundamentals for Non-HR Managers: Can We Be Friends? (& CYA!)

Partner with HR (and CYA)

HR would be thrilled if you create an environment on your team so that they will say positive things about the organization to others.

Start by looking at the career page of your company website. Look at how the job ads are worded. These are often the first things a job seeker will see and hence create the first impression. You'll be surprised at how often job postings make a company look unappealing!

Next — and frankly you'll want to brace yourself for this — check out what current and former employees say about your company on Glassdoor. These comments may be unduly negative because they are often made by disgruntled people who left the organization. However, it doesn't matter if the comments are fair. They are what people are reading about your company and it will affect who you can attract. Remember, the employment brand is about how people *perceive* the company; if those perceptions are inaccurate it can make hiring difficult.

As Author Kristen Hudson noted in her article, *Why Employer Branding is Critical in Attracting Top Talent*,

> "Today, employer brand is more important than ever, as nearly one-third of young people say they will preemptively reject a company with poor reviews…" [25]

Finally, it can be revealing to ask candidates what the perception of the company is amongst their peers. Since they are interviewing for a job, they are bound to be polite, but probe a little and you'll walk away with some insights. Having a sense of the employment brand will help you understand why you get the candidates you do after posting a job and will also help you understand what they are expecting when they come into the interview.

Who Is Responsible for the Employment Brand?

Usually HR has overall responsibility for the employment brand. They will work closely with marketing on this since the employment brand is a part of the overall company brand. If you are concerned that the employment brand is not suitable for attracting the right candidates, then you can talk to HR about it. They may not be able to change the career site for you, however they can tune the wording in the job posts for your department so that they project the right image.

Section 3 • Chapter 1 • Employment Branding: Isn't that the job of the Marketing Department?

71

Who else has responsibility for the employment brand? Have you guessed yet? It's you!

In practice, no matter what fancy pictures you put on a website, the true employment brand is rooted in the real experience of people working for the company. You have a good deal of control over what that experience is.

In fact, you may even be able to create a kind of mini-brand whereby your department has an excellent reputation even if the reputation of the company as a whole is only average. Make your department a place where people want to work.

Communicating your Own Mini-Brand

If you do a lot of hiring, you may have the opportunity to help create content for your career website that is specifically about your department. For example, if you manage the call center (and do a fabulous job if you do say so yourself) you might ask HR to include some videos of your happy team on the website. A candidate looking for a call center job will be particularly interested in hearing what current employees in that role say about their job.

Be sure to frame the conversation around the types of people that work on your team, their level of satisfaction, and how your team aligns with company goals. This information is valuable from a candidate perspective. Skip plain charts and details which can be meaningless to candidates or a big turn-off that might cause them to swipe left. Stick to what matters from a team perspective, including benefits, compensation, and what makes your workplace great.

Compliance Do's and Don'ts

- Do make sure that your messaging isn't biased towards or against certain groups. Double check the language.

Dealing with Negativity

From time to time, you probably need to address negativity and "BMW" (Berate, Moan, and Whine) among your team members. Remember that in today's world of social media, these comments may escape the workplace into the wild where they damage your employment brand.

As a manager, the best tactic is to listen and acknowledge that you understand their point of view. It's often the case that there is not much you can do about a complaint, but the good news is that people are often satisfied simply to have a manager who cares enough to listen.

It's also fair to tell employees that it's unprofessional of them to be constantly complaining about the company to their coworkers. If they genuinely don't like the overall deal they're getting (the employee value proposition), then they should move on rather than making the people around them miserable.

Let's hope it doesn't get to that; empathy and listening usually go a long way to nipping negativity in the bud.

Watch out for whiners. Deal with negativity before it gets out of hand.

Back to the Story

We're not sure about the fine points of employment contracts in Hell, but let's hope that, as in the real world, the woman was able to quit her job in Hell and apply again for that job driving angels around Heaven.

Your own reputation in the industry and community can be a powerful force in attracting talent.

Section 3 • Chapter 1 • Employment Branding: Isn't that the job of the Marketing Department?

73

Summing Up

Your ability to hire the right people is built on a partnership between both you, the hiring manager, and HR. You should recognize that:

- The organization's employment brand, how *the people you would like to hire* feel about your organization, matters to you since it affects the kinds of candidates who apply.

- The organization's employment value proposition, specifics like pay, benefits, and opportunities to advance your career, will help you close the deal with the candidate you want to hire.

- It's smart to get a sense of what candidates think about your company; you may feel it's great but what matters is their impression.

- Recognize that your own actions reflect on the organization's employment brand.

- Recognize that your own personal reputation or department's 'mini-brand' also have an impact on who will apply for open positions.

What is the reputation of your company? Ask around. Is it seen as a good place to work?

- Nothing will make your life easier than having the right team; that's why the time you take to build your recruiting skills is a good investment.

Let's do a quick practice activity on employment branding.

74

HR Fundamentals for Non-HR Managers: Can We Be Friends? (& CYA!)

Whose Swim Lane Is It?: Building Endurance in the Right Lane Activity

Think about how you and your team impact your employer brand and the steps you must take to build it. Then, look at the list of items in the **Whose Swim Lane?** box below. Place each item that is your responsibility in the **My Swim Lane** box. Place each item that is not your responsibility in the **Not My Swim Lane** box. For the items you placed in the 'Not My Swim Lane' box, who is responsible? Partner with those responsible in order to achieve the best outcomes for your team. How can you inspire your team to help improve and enhance your employer brand?

Whose Swim Lane?

Company messaging
Corporate footprint (social media)
Glassdoor/Indeed impressions (of management)
Team dynamics
Disgruntled employee complaints online
Reputation of my team
Reputation of my company
Community view of my company
Community view of my team
Industry perceptions of my company
Industry perceptions of me

My Swim Lane	Not My Swim Lane

Section 3 • Chapter 1 • Employment Branding: Isn't that the job of the Marketing Department?

75

RECRUITING THE RIGHT WAY

GET BIG TALENT ...NOT A BIG LAWSUIT

Key Terms and Definitions

Recruiting is the whole process of finding candidates and selecting one to fill a job vacancy.

Sourcing is the part of the process that finds candidates.

Bias refers to a range of human shortcomings that lead to poor hiring decisions.

The Issue

Do you need to fill some vacancies? That's easy; tell HR and they'll quickly deliver the ideal worker. If you believe that either you've got an extraordinary HR department or, buddy, you're new here, aren't you?

As a manager doing the hiring (what HR refers to as "the hiring manager"), you have a huge role to play in helping HR get you the right people.

A Short Story

"Actually, I don't even know why I was invited to this interview," said Celine.

The IT manager had to agree. She had expertise in NXP 3.1, and the existing system was NXP 2.8. There's no way a 3.1'er would want to work in a 2.8'er shop. Surely HR knows this, he thought.

The job had been open for months and HR either sent overqualified candidates, underqualified candidates or candidates with a mismatched skill set. It was almost as if no one in HR had spent a day in their lives managing an IT function.

All the interviewing was taking too much of the IT manager's time and he often had to postpone the interviews at the last minute. There was one candidate who he had to postpone three times! She looked good on paper, but he couldn't be sure because she had politely declined the next invitation to an interview.

76

HR Fundamentals for Non-HR Managers: Can We Be Friends? (& CYA!)

> **Partner with HR (and CYA)**
>
> For legal reasons, HR needs you to stick to the script of what you can and cannot say in an interview. Furthermore, HR is counting on you to be professional in playing your role in the process (e.g. don't take a phone call in an interview).

Clearly, HR was messing up and the IT manager didn't know what to do about it.

Understanding the Recruitment Process

There is a big distinction in recruiting between regular recruiting and high-volume recruiting. If your organization is doing high-volume recruiting, hiring hundreds of people into a particular job each year, then it'll be a fine-tuned process that runs like any other efficient supply chain. For these jobs, while the hiring manager does have distinct responsibilities, HR will do most of the heavy lifting.

Regular recruiting occurs when the organization hires only a few people, maybe only one person, for a given role every year. In regular recruiting, HR may need a lot more help from the hiring manager to get it right—especially if it is a specialized role. In this chapter, we'll focus mainly on regular recruiting.

It's a good idea to think of recruitment as a six-step process. Let's put them in order:

❶ Create the job description

Does that sound painful and bureaucratic? A lot of managers think so and so they just find an old job description at the bottom of a drawer and shoot it over to HR. How well is a recruiter going to be able to find the right person if they're working from an out-of-date document that doesn't reflect what you need?

Rather than think, "I need to write a job description," think, "I need to figure out what is needed in this role and then communicate that to HR in a way that makes sense to them." This can be surprisingly difficult if you haven't done it before. This is a good time to partner with HR. Have a conversation with them about what the job is and the kind of person you're looking for. That conversation will make a big difference in helping you document what you need so that HR can begin the recruiting process.

Key point: It's the manager's job to communicate accurately to HR what is needed in the role.

"What's an appropriate salary???"

Key point: The company will have a process for selecting the appropriate pay range; they will need accurate information from you about the role to do so.

③ Sourcing

Next comes sourcing. What is "sourcing" you ask? It's the word recruiters use to describe getting candidates to apply for the job opening. It starts with the thing we talked about in the previous chapter: the employment brand. The employment brand helps ensure people are interested in applying for a job at your organization. More directly related to the opening you need to fill now, HR will start advertising the job and/or use 'direct sourcing' to find candidates.

Advertising typically means posting the job on your organization's career site and job boards. There are lots of ways to advertise including putting up posters in bus stops. You don't need to worry about this much, as HR (or a third-party firm HR has hired) will handle this.

② Determine the compensation range

In most cases, the pay range for the job will already be self-evident (hint: it will be the same as the last person in the job). However, if it's a new job, then the organization will need to decide what the appropriate pay grade is for that kind of work. They'll have a process for that. The more clarity you can give them about what you need the more likely the process will end with an appropriate pay grade.

Direct sourcing means seeking out specific individuals, usually by searching LinkedIn or other online sources, to look for people with the right qualifications. Direct sourcing is used for more senior roles and for professional roles that are hard to fill. This approach is often described as searching for "passive candidates," that is people who are not actively looking for work. It's often believed that the best people are already happily employed elsewhere and so you need to seek them out; they won't be looking at job ads.

Employee referral programs, where you ask employees to recommend people they know for an opening, can be considered a kind of direct sourcing. Usually these programs offer a payment to the employee who makes a recommendation that leads to a successful hire. Again, you don't have to worry about that too much, HR (or a third-party firm HR has hired) will handle this. However, you should ask your employees to participate in such a program since referrals often lead to getting high quality new hires who fit the culture.

> Ask your team to refer good people to fill job vacancies.

Key point: HR generally handles sourcing; we will talk about your own personal brand and how that can play a role in sourcing at the end of this chapter.

4 Screening and short-listing

Are you getting excited about actually seeing some candidates? Well, hold on, there's another set of steps. HR will probably end up with many applicants for the job and they'll have processes for taking that long list and turning it into a shortlist.

If you are lucky, HR will have a sophisticated system for shortlisting, quite possibly involving assessment tests or pre-screening calls from a recruiter. If you are unlucky, HR's screening and short-listing process will be to dump 100 resumes on your desk and ask you who you want to interview. Going through those resumes is a tough job and in truth, it's hard to know from a quick look at a resume who the best candidates will be.

Here's an idea. Why don't you put off looking at those resumes and get to it later? Sounds pretty sweet!

OK, here's the problem. Somewhere in that pile of resumes are strong candidates and they have applied to several jobs. They are going to take the first enticing offer, and if you've delayed the process then by the time you get around to asking them for an interview they'll be long gone.

The process most experienced managers follow is to take a quick look at a resume and put it in one of three piles "Yes," "Maybe," or "No." At the end of the first sort, if you have too many in the "Yes" pile you take a second pass and narrow it down. If you don't have enough in the "Yes" pile, take a second look at the "Maybes."

In the unlikely case that you don't have any suitable candidates, then it's time to book a meeting with HR so that you can (no, not so you can yell at them) work together to figure out how to attract a better set of candidates.

Key point: If you are involved in short-listing, don't put it off. Do a quick scan of the resumes sorting them into "Yes," "Maybe" and "No" piles.

5 Scheduling interviews

Why does scheduling interviews rate the status of a full step in the process? It's because it's an area where hiring managers (like you) often mess up. HR has the short-list and asks you to find time to interview them. Trouble is, you're one heck of a busy person so it's hard to find time for those interviews.

You might even think, "My job is running this department not filling vacancies." How wrong you are! A crucial part of your job is bringing in new talent. Invest time and effort in filling those vacancies, and it will pay off big time.

The bottom line here: Get those

> The candidate can't be late for the interview. Neither can you.

candidates scheduled for interviews as soon as possible. That gives you your best chance of getting great people before they're snatched up elsewhere.

Key point: Prioritize moving the hiring process along quickly, or it will come back to bite you.

6 Conducting one or more interviews

This is really where the rubber hits the road. Here, you should partner with HR since they will know a lot about how to conduct an effective (and legal) interview. You will know a lot about the specific skills you need for the role. Work with HR so that you have good interviews. Ask for their advice. Listen to their opinions. Heed their warnings.

Key point: Strive to learn interviewing skills. Ask HR to help. Follow their lead. Take it seriously, nothing affects your success more than the quality of your team.

Good (and bad) Interview Questions

Before we talk about beautiful interview questions, let's get the ugly topic of bad questions out of the way. By "bad" we really mean "illegal." Is it okay to ask a young woman, "When do you expect to start having babies?" No, it's not okay and there's a good chance it is illegal (it varies by legal jurisdiction). HR will be *more* than happy to tell you about which questions you cannot ask. Please have a conversation with HR about what you can't ask. Remember, they are not just making up these rules for fun; they are telling you what is out-and-out against the law or a clear violation of company policy.

Here are the types of questions HR will tell you **not** to ask:

- How many children do you have and what ages are they? (Even if you provide onsite daycare, this is for HR to discuss with the individual if the person is hired and needs this benefit.)

- So, what do you like doing on the weekends? (Sounds innocuous, but if they participate in religious, political, ethnic, or familial events, this could provide a basis for a discrimination claim if they do not get hired.)

- You're engaged! Great! When do you think you will start a family? (No. Just, no. You may be trying to be friendly, but this information is irrelevant to the position, and can also be used against you if the person is not hired.)

- You mentioned that you will need non-fluorescent lighting for your migraines. As you know, we have unlimited PTO, but roughly how many days a month do you anticipate needing to be off?

> For better results, follow a structured interviewing process where you ask each candidate the same questions.

(Cannot ask this or any version of this question.)

Now on a more positive note, what **can** you ask? More effective questions to ask include:

- What are your career goals?

- In what ways do our company and this role align with those goals?

- What is prompting a move at this time?

- What are the successes you have achieved and are most proud of?

- What is an example of having "missed the mark" on an

assignment? What did you do, how did you rectify it, what did you learn?

- Do you like managing the tasks of the project or managing people in performing those tasks?

After each answer, probe to get more details. You should try to get as specific answers as possible; aim to find out exactly what they did, not just a general version. If someone says they "researched this issue," ask specifically what research they did. Furthermore, ask about the context so that you can judge the answer more accurately.

You can also ask some questions to get to know them better:

- What types of training and certificates are you hoping to get in the next year or two?

- Are you currently being mentored for broadening or elevating your career? If not, what are some elements that you would consider helpful in your mentorship?

- In what ways do you feel that you will need the most coaching?

- How do you feel you can coach or train others?

- Do you have a timeframe in mind for advancement, and what would that look like for you?

Other Aspects of Effective Interviewing

We'll look at interviewing again in the next chapter, but for now, let's just point out a few useful tips:

- Talk about the job and the company but not so much that you run out of time to interview the candidate (e.g. keep it to 10-15 minutes in a 60-minute interview).

- Leave time for the candidate to ask questions. It is often the case that these lead to insights into the person and help you both decide if the job is a good fit. (e.g. set aside 15-20 minutes in a 60-minute interview).

- Prepare a list of questions in advance and ask each candidate the same questions. This is called a "structured interview" and it leads to better results and less bias.

How Many Interviews Should You Have?

Companies can organize the interviewing process in many different ways. Some do one-on-one interviews, and some do panels (where there are several interviewers at one time). Some do many interviews (10 or more is not unheard of), and some only do one.

What's the right process? It depends on the job and the company culture, but here are a few general tips:

- Two (or three) heads are better than one. Get multiple people to be part of the interviewing process and listen to all their opinions.

82

HR Fundamentals for Non-HR Managers: Can We Be Friends? (& CYA!)

- Relying on just one interview is risky. Someone may seem great (or mediocre) in one interview. Maybe they were just having a good/bad day. Maybe it was just *you* having a good/bad day. Hiring is such an important decision that you need a second look.

- Having many interviews stretches out the process over time (which can cause you to lose candidates), can be exhausting for candidates (which they resent) and it also eats up a lot of management time. Google used to be famous for having many interviews until finally, HR took a closer look and the data analytics revealed what you already know: it's stupid to put someone through a dozen interviews.

Compliance Do's and Don'ts

- You MUST be aware of fair hiring legislation and what you cannot ask in an interview. Do sit down with HR to learn what's needed in your area.

The Role of Bias

If we tell you that you're biased, you may think we are saying you are a terrible human. That's not it at all; we are simply saying you *are* a human. Bias is just a part of how our brain works and it includes things like paying more attention to what happened recently (e.g. what someone said at the end of the interview) rather than taking a balanced perspective on the whole interview.

Choosing the wrong candidate due to predisposed biases is an expensive mistake. (Got money to burn?!) The decision can be way more costly to your company than you might think. For example, should you have to train a replacement due to a biased hire, your team's productivity and morale may be negatively affected. (Tornado Warning: Take cover!) Additionally, there will be a cost to the company for sourcing, hiring, and training the replacement employee. On the other hand, making a suitable, unbiased hire can help establish a culture of high performance and excellence on your team.

Reducing bias and increasing fairness and validity in hiring practices can, therefore, increase your retention rate so you won't need a ball and chain to keep employees around. Furthermore, many biases violate state and federal employment regulations; let's do all we can to reduce bias.

Common Cognitive Biases

Clifton and Harter explain the type of biases that can affect the hiring process and we have added examples after each:

Glare factors: Hiring managers give disproportionate weight to characteristics that appear on the surface during an interview, such as how candidates look, dress and present themselves.

Example: A candidate walked into the room dripping wet and appeared to be utterly disheveled. Reason? His car broke down a mile away, and he ran the rest of the way to arrive as close to the interview time as possible.

Experience fallacy: Hiring managers had an applicant from a previous employer turn out to be highly successful, so they assume everyone from that company will be successful.

Example: Because it is "XYZ" Corporation, right? And they're known for their stringent vetting process. Remember that "just because" is not a reason to give this candidate more weight.

Your gut feel is probably biased. Pay attention to the evidence.
#FactBasedDecisions

Overconfidence bias: Hiring managers believe that they have a special ability to judge applicants based on their gut and don't consider other information.

Example: You always go with your gut because it has served you every single time... except this one time. There is a first time for everything!

Similarity bias: Hiring managers select and hire people who are like them.

Example: There are hundreds of examples, but this is why you need to have more than one person involved in the hiring decision! Seek to have people with a variety of perspectives, skills, experience so that you get a well rounded view of the candidate. This will help you to "check" yourself.

Stereotype bias: Hiring managers have unconscious stereotypes associated with gender, race, sexual orientation, ethnicity, and age.

Example: Gray hair (like yours from the stress of hiring!) A person's appearance can communicate many things to hiring managers. You may assume the person is digitally challenged, on heart medication, won't "fit in," or will turn out like "Edith," who never participated in "Casual Friday," and people felt uncomfortable with her "clutching her pearls" mode.

Availability bias: Hiring managers rely on their memory of an interview and make a decision based on a few high or low points rather than taking a comprehensive view.

Example: Four candidates were scheduled back to back. You didn't take copious notes. You even forgot which one mastered the Python programming language. Without detailed notes, your brain simply retrieves the most readily available impressions and you go with that.

Escalation of commitment: Hiring managers feel pressured to move forward with a candidate because they have already invested so much time or energy in the process.

Example: Especially for billable contracts where, for every day that someone is not working is a day of lost revenue for the company. This has now devolved into a "butts in seats" proposition, and everyone loses.

Confirmation bias: Hiring managers form a distinct impression of a candidate based on the school they attended or a club they belonged to and only hear comments that confirm their beliefs about the person.

> If someone makes a good first impression, you tend to (foolishly) ignore facts that contradict this. It's called confirmation bias.

Example: One's college alma mater and fraternity/sorority contain individual students/members. Each person is not defined by these alliances no matter what the "general rule of thumb" may be affiliated with regards to the reputations of said universities/groups. [26]

Because of these biases, it's not unusual for managers to make hiring decisions they later regret after actually spending time with the person on the job.

How To Reduce Cognitive Bias

Other than turning you into a robot, there is no way we can eliminate bias. However, there are three things you can do to reduce bias:

- Write down a list of the biases you are most concerned about and bring those with you into the interview. When you reflect on the interview, take a look at the biases to see if any might be distorting your judgment.

- Invite several people to be part of your interview team, and ask them to also keep an eye out for bias.

- Make greater use of assessments. There are many well-validated assessment tools that can give you unbiased data to help inform your decision.

Pay attention to your biases and you will gradually improve.

You can take this to the next level by elevating your "manager brand" which is your own personal version of an employment brand. Speak at conferences, write articles, and post items on LinkedIn to raise your visibility. Join community organizations both as a source of contacts and as a way to demonstrate that you are the kind of person who gives back. Pay attention to the impression you are making on people, how professional you look, whether you sound knowledgeable, appear friendly, or if you sound like you're listening and interested.

As a manager who wants the best team, there is a lot you can take into your own hands so that you become a great partner to HR.

Your Personal Manager Brand (Yes you may want to play a special role!)

There is one last point we want to raise. You can do a lot of sourcing (finding potential candidates) on your own. This is especially important if you are in a specialized field. If you are a finance manager, go to networking events outside your company and keep an eye open for the kind of people you would like to hire one day. If job hunters ask to meet you, consider having an informal informational meeting just to get to know them even if you don't have an opening right now. Keep in touch with the talented people you meet by connecting on LinkedIn so you can get in touch when you do have an opening.

86

HR Fundamentals for Non-HR Managers: Can We Be Friends? (& CYA!)

Back to the Story

Our IT manager was frustrated with HR when the source of the problem could be found in the mirror. An HR professional is unlikely to have deep insight into the technical skills that the manager needs, especially since the required skills are always changing. As a manager, you will have more success with hiring if you make every effort to help HR understand exactly what you need.

Summing Up

Let's review the most important points:

- It's important that managers understand the six steps in the recruitment process and the role they are expected to play.

- The manager is particularly important in the interview stage. It's important to learn the skills of interviewing so that you give candidates a good impression of the organization, learn what you need to know about them, and avoid asking anything illegal!

- One special area of concern is bias.

If you are not getting great candidates, then you need to ask the recruiter why that is happening and figure out a solution.

There is no magic pill to eliminate bias, however you should be conscious of possible biases and take steps to minimize them.

- A particular strategy some managers have adopted is to build a personal "manager brand" that complements the organization's employment brand. Managers who have a good network of people, who are always on the lookout for talent, and have a strong reputation will find it much easier to fill vacancies with top caliber employees.

Now let's deepen our understanding of recruitment with an exercise.

Building Your Recruiting Strategy Activity

Think briefly about your personal reputation in your profession. Now take time to complete a personal inventory checklist by answering each question provided in the Inventory Box. Then, think of a position for which you may need to hire in the future. Write a job description in the Job Description Box that will attract the right candidates.

	Inventory
1	What would those in my social circles say about me as a participant in social events?
Answer	
2	How would others describe my demeanor during rush hour traffic?
Answer	
3	Would my team members say that I am patient? Fair? Supportive?
Answer	
4	Am I a manager or a leader?
Answer	
5	How do my behaviors in my personal life reflect upon my professional life?
Answer	

88

HR Fundamentals for Non-HR Managers: Can We Be Friends? (& CYA!)

Job Description	
1	Make a list of duties. Describe what it looks like on your team to do those duties for a specific job. How can you write each description to intrigue and engage candidates?
Duties:	
2	Write out a list of qualifications for the role. Ask yourself the question, "Why is this quality or skill required? Is it really necessary to have the listed education?"
Answer:	
3	What can the person performing in this job expect for growth opportunities?
Answer:	
4	Why would the successful candidate "want" to work on your team?
Answer:	

An additional activity:

Ask HR or your Recruiter to give you ten prospective candidates to reach out to with some guidelines on personalizing an email to each of them. If the potential candidates do not respond, try other ways to email. Then, try calling and/or texting. Note how many attempts at contact you must make in order to reach a candidate via email, or by phone, text message, connect request on LinkedIn, or any of the other ways that candidates are recruited by your company. This will enable you to understand the effort and activities that must go into recruiting for your team! (Exasperated yet?)

CANDIDATE EXPERIENCE

ENSURE THE HIRING PROCESS IS A POSITIVE ONE

Key Terms and Definitions

Candidate experience –
How candidates feel as they go through the process of applying for a job with your organization.

The Issue

In the first two chapters of this section, we have been viewing recruitment largely from the company's point of view. Here we turn the tables and ask what the recruitment experience is like for the candidates who apply to work with you. An enjoyable candidate experience will make it more likely that the top candidate will accept your offer. It will also make it more likely that the candidates who did not get an offer will speak well of the organization and recommend it to their friends (remember your Employment Brand!). A poor candidate experience will… well I expect you can guess how that impacts the employment brand!

A Short Story

Phil, the Manager of a design team at an illustration and graphics company, was expanding his team and interviewing new candidates. In debriefing with some candidates, HR discovered that they came away disillusioned, confused, or disappointed. More than a few said that while they appreciated being considered, the company wasn't a "good fit" and they were dropping out of the process.

The complaints varied from candidate to candidate. One felt it was unfair when Phil said, "You're a job hopper, aren't you?," when he should have understood that it was the nature of the federal contracts he worked on. Another was unhappy that Phil took a call in the middle of an interview. A third said that she was told she'd hear back about next steps in a couple of days, but weeks had passed with no contact. "Your company ghosted me," she sighed.

Partner with HR (and CYA)

If you treat candidates the way you would treat a customer and how you would want to be treated, then you've played your role in creating candidate engagement.

HR asked Phil about this and he had loads of reasons why those things had happened. He also pointed out to HR that there were lots of fish in the sea; he was sure that he would get the job filled so no big deal.

Is it a big deal? Let's think about how we should approach the candidate experience.

What is the Candidate Experience?

Candidate experience is a broad term about how candidates feel as they go through the process of applying for a job with your organization. Companies — including yours — want their potential employees to have positive interactions when auditioning for a role on their teams. This includes the complete experience from visiting the career website through to the application and interview processes.

Does Candidate Experience Really Matter?

Every individual who interacts with your company is not just a candidate, but potentially a new employee, a referrer of potential hires and maybe even a customer. Treat a candidate well and that creates a positive vibe that emanates out over time. Treat candidates poorly and you can be sure they'll be talking about it for years.

In the article, *What is Candidate Engagement?* TalentLyft writes,

> In various surveys, the majority of job seekers...60%... have indicated they received poor treatment during their job search...A CareerBuilder survey found that when job seekers have a bad candidate experience, 42%... would never apply to that company again and 22%...would tell other candidates not to work at that company. [27]

Let's look at the case of Virgin Media. In 2016, Graeme Johnson presented at LinkedIn's TalentConnect conference on his findings about the impact of a bad candidate experience. Virgin Media discovered that many candidates were so annoyed that they canceled their subscriptions to Virgin Media products. Johnson estimated those bad experiences cost the company at least 7,400 customers or $5.8 million in revenue. (Holy smokes!)

Sometimes you'll hear HR say we should treat candidates like customers. Well, Virgin Media discovered they *really were* customers! No matter what your business is, it makes sense to have enough discipline to create a pleasant candidate experience. As a manager, you play a big role in that.

Where the Experience Starts

The candidate experience begins when a candidate first researches your company online.

- Is the website engaging? Does it align with the kind of place they'd like to work? Is it easy for them to find their way around?

- When they hit the career page, does it have the information a candidate wants? Can they navigate to the information they need?

- When they go to apply, is the process simple or cumbersome? Does it take too much time? Does it require them to re-type information that is already in their resume?

Ask your candidates whether the application process was cumbersome.

It's HR's job to make sure that the start of the experience goes smoothly for the candidate. It's not a bad idea for you as a manager to try out the process to see what the candidates you want to hire have to go through to get as far as applying. If it's the kind of experience that will turn off qualified candidates, then talk to HR and support them when they say they need the resources to upgrade the experience.

First Impressions

Imagine the candidate who could be a great worker for you. Imagine the cheery smile they bring to the office. Imagine how productive they are. Imagine how your boss gets up at the annual corporate meeting and interrupts the Chairman of the Board to point out that you are just 'the most fabulous manager ever' because of the excellent hire you made...ah we can dream can't we?

Now imagine the first impression that candidate gets when they walk in for the interview and begin sizing up the company. Are they greeting politely? Did the receptionist acknowledge that they were expected? Were they offered a drink? Is the reception area attractive? Is it cool?

Now consider the first impression they have of you. Are you friendly? Punctual? Well-organized?

In this meeting, it's not just you assessing them; it's them assessing you.

First impressions are something you have a lot of control over and it's your responsibility to make sure you don't blow it—or, to put it more kindly, that you have an opportunity to land a candidate who otherwise would have gone elsewhere - by making a great first impression.

This is an opportunity for you to partner with HR. Tell them what you think about the first impression that is being created. Get their thoughts on it. Work together to make things better.

The Interview from the Candidate's Perspective

The main point of an interview is for you to assess the candidate's fit for the job. However, the whole idea of candidate experience is that we should look at things not just from our own perspective but from the candidate's perspective as well. What are your interviews like for the candidate?

Here are some things to check:

- Are there times where the candidates may feel your questions are unfair?

Interviews should be enjoyable for the candidate.

- Are there times when they may think your comments are discouraging or inappropriate?

- Do you take the time to acknowledge their previous accomplishments, and recognize them for the experiences they can add to your team? Remember, we all appreciate praise (even you — come on, admit it)!

- Do you thank them for coming in? Do you thank them for their time at the end of the interview?

- Do you let them know (realistically) when they'll hear back?

Remember even if it is quickly evident

that this is not an ideal candidate, you want them to leave the process ready to tell people how much they liked the company, how they thought you'd be a great boss, and why someone who is an ideal candidate really should take the time to apply for a job with you.

Note that these guidelines apply whether the interview is in person, by phone or by video conference. Some people are still uncomfortable on video so make allowances for that. Also, it's still quite common for people to have technical difficulties with video conferences, so make sure you are set up to handle those, and if they do occur make sure you put the person at ease after the difficulty is corrected. Don't let technical difficulties get in the way of identifying the best talent.

Wining, Dining, and Touring

If a candidate looks like a good fit, it's common to enhance their experience by giving them a tour of the company and taking them out for lunch or dinner. This is an opportunity for you and the candidate to get to know each other better as real human beings.

- Do be professional and respectful.

- Don't tell off-color jokes or do anything that could be perceived as harassment.

The reason this problem occurs so often is that stuff happens; everyone gets super busy and the recruitment process gets put on the backburner. The company doesn't get back to the candidate with news because there is no news—literally the company hasn't thought about it at all in the weeks after the interview because they've been so buried in other work.

Take a moment to think about this aspect of the candidate experience. Are you putting in that extra bit of effort to show you care? Does it feel authentic to you? Remember, if you find the process uncomfortable, they probably do too, so figure out a new approach.

One last piece of advice: provide final candidates with the ability to interact with some current employees. With you, they are dealing with a boss-subordinate relationship which introduces a certain formality. With current employees, they will be talking to peers. That's something candidates will appreciate.

After the Process

Have you ever heard of a case where someone interviewed with a company, and then weeks passed without them hearing anything at all? We bet you have, because it happens all the time. Now use your powers of deep analysis: how does that make the candidate feel?

94

HR Fundamentals for Non-HR Managers: Can We Be Friends? (& CYA!)

Okay, let's make an important change to that last sentence. It's not "the company" who didn't get back to them, it's "you." This is your team; you are the manager; this is your personal reputation as a well-organized and thoughtful leader. It is your responcibility to send them a note with your apologies, letting them know why the process is being delayed, and acking if they have any questions.

Personalizing the Experience

If you are doing a lot of hiring, it may be tempting to call in the person by announcing, "Candidate number 6742, please report to the interviewing room." That's a temptation to avoid. Make sure you look at the person's name before you meet

them. If you're unsure of how to pronounce it, ask them (you might even get them to help you write it out phonetically if you struggle when pronouncing uncommon names). Try to use their name in the interview. When you communicate with them, as much as possible add in some unique comments, rather than just sending out a templated message.

Small things? Yes, but they make a difference.

Top Tier Candidate Experience Elsewhere

For optimal candidate engagement, candidates should be treated like customers.

> Every candidate is a special individual, even when you have dozens of candidates.

> The best candidates have other options so treat them well.

Remember, top tier candidates are probably being given a personalized experience elsewhere, so you really need to bring your A-game and do the same. Most candidates with whom you are interacting are simultaneously in conversations with other companies and can be influenced in one direction or another, in part based on their candidate experience.

Now, more than ever, a generic, universal process may cause you to miss out on talent! As you know, one size never fits all — the same can be said about the candidate engagement experience. Hone your candidate engagement and work with HR/Leadership to ensure compliance. Ultimately, your approach to candidate engagement will help you attract the right candidates to build the team you want.

Back to the Story

There are a lot of things you need to learn to be a successful manager. Phil clearly had not yet learned the role he had to play in bringing in the best people onto his team. As a result, his own performance would suffer (due to a weak team) and he was hurting the company's reputation.

Luckily, Phil's weaknesses are easily corrected. We like to believe he will read this chapter, take it to heart, and begin creating a great candidate experience.

Summing Up

When we begin the hiring process, we normally see it through the lens of our own needs. What do we want? What's convenient for us? The concept of candidate experience reminds us that we should pay attention to how the process feels for the candidate.

Here are some of the key ideas:

- Candidate experience matters because a good experience makes it more likely that top candidates will accept your offer and that even rejected candidates will speak well of your company in the future. Candidate experience can even affect sales, especially in companies selling consumer products.

- Unfortunately, many companies do a poor job of managing the candidate experience (translation: they treat candidates like dirt).

96

HR Fundamentals for Non-HR Managers: Can We Be Friends? (& CYA!)

- The candidate experience starts when the candidate first starts researching your company, in particular when they first visit the career page and consider applying. HR and/or Marketing are responsible for the career page.

- You can make a difference in checking that candidates get a positive first impression when they come in for an interview.

- You can make an even bigger difference by making sure the interview process is professional, feels fair, and is (to the extent possible) an enjoyable experience for all candidates.

- Most candidates will be rejected. Often companies neglect to tell people that they have been rejected or put on hold. Insist that HR keep all candidates aware of their status or do it yourself.

While HR does have a key role to play, hiring is a partnership and it's an area where a manager should work closely with HR. Beyond that, the manager should do everything in their power to ensure an enjoyable candidate experience. This is not something that takes a lot of time or money; it just requires that managers understand the importance of the candidate experience so that they do the little things that make a difference.

The little things include knowing the candidate's name, treating them politely in the interview, and getting back to them when you said you would (even if it is simply to say that the process is running behind schedule). You don't need to take time off to get a PhD in candidate experience; this is just 'Being a Human 101."

Now spend a moment on an activity that will give you insights on what an engaging candidate interview looks like.

> Even candidates who don't get the job offer should walk away feeling they love your company.

Sell Me This Pen...NOT! Selling vs. Engaging Activity

Think about the candidate's interview experience in its present form. In the **Selling Column**, list the steps presently in place that lean towards "selling" or "enticing" candidates to join your team. In the **Engaging Column**, list the things you can start doing on your team to enhance the candidate's experience in the interview. Try doing this activity with those you collaborate with to recruit, interview, and hire candidates. You can refer back to this activity after you have implemented some changes and update it to see how your tactics have evolved.

Selling	Engaging
e.g. "We have great benefits" e.g. "You'll learn a lot here"	e.g. "How does this position align with your career goals?" e.g. "Is there something about this company you find particularly appealing?"

98

HR Fundamentals for Non-HR Managers: Can We Be Friends? (& CYA!)

SECTION 4

Onboarding and Orientation:
You've got one chance to
make a first impression

WELCOME AND ORIENTATION

GETTING NEW HIRES OFF ON THE RIGHT FOOT

Effective onboarding can ramp up assimilation of your new hire to your team, reducing turnover costs.

Key Terms and Definitions

Orientation – The mechanics of getting a person started (e.g. HR paperwork, security passes).

Onboarding – Getting people feeling like part of the team and then becoming a productive member of that team.

The Issue

There are a couple of things that can go wrong when an employee first joins a company. One is that the employee does not feel properly welcomed. For example, if they arrive and they don't have the necessary equipment, then they'll feel that they are not valued (and they may also feel the company doesn't care about doing things the right way).

The other thing that can go wrong is if the new employee isn't properly integrated into their work so that they don't get much done in the first few months. That has an immediate cost: you are paying for an unproductive employee. It also can have a longer term cost: the employee decides that the company doesn't care about productivity.

You can avoid these problems by putting in place a solid orientation and onboarding process.

A Short Story

Maria was super excited to start her new job at Widgets, Inc. and on day one she seemed to be off to a great start. She arrived, as instructed, at 8am sharp. The office manager escorted her to her new cubicle where — to her delight and surprise — everything was already set up. In addition to a name plate on her cubicle **(nice!),** she found a box of ready-made business cards **(sweet!)** and a binder with directions on how to set up her office phone voice mail. Captured in a personalized manual, she also found the network login codes for her PC so she could get her email set up and find various company directories. Her desk was outfitted with folders, notepads, pens, and a coffee mug all emblazoned with the company logo and "#1 Team" printed on it. Once logged in, Maria checked her calendar and saw a few meetings already scheduled for later in the week, as well as a welcome lunch scheduled for Friday. "Wow!" She felt like she was flying high with such a great company!

By 10am, the office was buzzing! Phones were ringing, people were chatting, and several folks had stopped by to say "Hello" and introduce themselves. By 11:30am, Maria had read through every page of the company intranet and organized her desk. She started to look forward to lunch. Her onboarding manual contained a handy guide (with helpful maps) listing all of the restaurants within walking distance of the office. After eating lunch alone, Maria returned to her desk and scrolled through the intranet until it was time to leave. Tuesday and Wednesday were the same.

"How are you liking the new job?" Maria's roommate asked her on Wednesday night. "The people are great; very friendly for sure. Of course, they all know each other and I'm the newbie. I'm actually looking forward to Friday for my welcome lunch. Maybe then I'll start to feel like I'm part of the group," she answered. "Of course," she added, "I don't really know what to do yet. I hope I'll get some direction at our meeting tomorrow."

"What about your manager?" her roommate asked, "isn't anyone showing you the ropes and training you?"

"Well," shrugged Maria, "we have a team lead who's in charge of that but she's on vacation this week. I imagine I'll get some direction when she comes back next week."

Partner with HR (and CYA)

Follow a checklist of orientation and onboarding steps. In particular, be well prepared the first day someone new arrives at work. (Don't be surprised on the day they show up!)

Onboarding is mainly about getting people feeling like part of the team and then becoming a productive member of that team. It includes introductions, some tasks to get started, some longer term objectives, any necessary training, and possibly a buddy who will help them get acclimatized in the first couple of months. In this chapter, we'll focus on the socialization side of onboarding and get to the 'becoming productive' side in the next chapter.

"I guess the coffee mug and t-shirt were nice touches, but they sure seemed to have dropped the ball on the socialization aspect," the roommate pointed out.

"Maybe so," said Maria. "I hope when I connect with the team I'll start to really feel like they want me there".

Making a Distinction Between Orientation and Onboarding

It's useful to make a distinction between onboarding and orientation (one of these things is not like the other). Orientation is mainly about the mechanics of getting a person started. It includes getting their HR paperwork done, giving them appropriate passwords and security badges, making sure they know the basic rules (start time, break time, end time), and of course, the location of the restrooms! Most of this is usually handled in their first day or two on the job.

YES YOU

Who is Responsible for Orientation and Onboarding?

Most managers would say HR is responsible for orientation and onboarding. The reality is that both HR and the manager have big roles to play. HR is responsible for taking new hires through their new employee paperwork and enrolling them in everything from I-9, payroll, and benefits to their 401(k) retirement plans. It is your job, as the manager, to ensure that your new hire is properly onboarded to your team. Pick your jaw up. It'll be okay, we promise! In real life, there is more to them than their resumes! This is a great time to discover all the hidden treasures in your new hire.

The Cost of Not Getting It Right

While you, no doubt, agree--in theory--that clarity and two-way communication are good things; it can be hard to fit into a busy schedule. Does it really matter if we skip or delay those onboarding conversations? What happens when the onboarding process goes wrong?

ClearCompany points out that,

> ...(SHRM) estimates that 69% of employees are more likely to remain in a company for three years when they have had a good quality onboarding experience. Not only will they stay, but they will also be more productive. In fact, organizations that have an excellent onboarding process will experience 50% greater new hire productivity. [28]

Costly turnover can result from poor onboarding, so it's important to cross the t's and dot the i's! In fact, it is believed that, on average — if the onboarding process is poor — hourly workers will leave a company roughly four months after joining, while salaried employees will leave after just eighteen months.

This fact is supported by Online Manager and Editor of Talent Acquisition for SHRM Roy Maurer's Society for Human Resource Management blog article, *Employers Risk Driving New Hires Away with Poor Onboarding*, as he shared,

Lack of onboarding leads to lower productivity.

> "Employers report that the absence of an onboarding process leads to lower productivity, higher employee turnover and lower employee engagement," said Chris Lennon, vice president of product management at BirdDogHR, a talent management software and services provider based in Des Moines, Iowa. [29]

This isn't scary at all, is it?!

Given the cost of poor onboarding, do managers ever get it wrong? You betcha. How many jobs have you started where you experienced technical issues on the first day? How often have you had trouble accessing shared folders, cloud workspaces, and company directories as a new employee? Remember how frustrating that was? (Face-palm!)

A poor orientation and onboarding process is a common and costly problem. If you take some simple actions you can avoid that problem. Let's start by spending a moment explaining how you can make sure that orientation is on track.

Orientation: You Need To Be in the Know

There is a good chance that the mechanics of orientation (e.g. filling in HR forms, getting a PC) will be beautifully coordinated by HR. If it's not, whose fault is that? Well, we won't get far by assigning blame. A better question is "Who suffers?" It's your employee, your team, and you who suffer if orientation doesn't go well.

It's your job as a manager to understand what happens in the orientation program. Ask HR to explain the process they follow. If there are any gaps, then it's up to you to fill them.

Creating That Lovin' Feeling

There is a results-oriented side to onboarding (here is what you need to achieve) and a social side (you are a valued member of a team). Once the new team member has arrived and completed the basic orientation, it is time to bring out the welcome wagon. Be careful to not run anyone over because, you know, safety and all that.

First, make sure you know how they want to be addressed (ie. first name, middle name, nickname). If there is any doubt, find out if they should be addressed as "he," "she" or something else. Make sure you can pronounce their name. Don't hesitate to say, "Just give me a minute to write this out phonetically" and get them to help you get it right.

Second, pick an appropriate way to formally announce the arrival of your new team member. For example, you could assemble everyone in your department for introductions and welcomes, or have a remote welcome meeting if your team works remotely. A great ice breaker activity is to have each person share a funny story about their first day or week on your team. This will go a long way in helping your new hire connect and feel less anxious in their new environment.

Third, introduce them to a buddy or mentor. The buddy/mentor is simply someone who they can go to who will help them get settled. It's kind of like telling the new hire, "If you've got a question that you're not comfortable asking me, then ask your buddy." The buddy/mentor can be anyone in your department who has been around long enough to know the ropes and enjoys helping a new hire.

> It helps to give new hires a buddy who can show them the ropes.

Here are additional ways to welcome them:

- A department-wide message sharing a little bit about the new team member, their role, and something quirky they feel comfortable sharing

- Virtual welcome greetings by teammates who are not in the office

- An office tour where people are wearing name badges

- An agenda for the first week including meetings with people they should know (for example, a short meeting with your boss)

- A list of names, roles, phone numbers, and email addresses of team members

- A "What to do when" guide and "Who to call" tips (not Ghostbusters!)

Mission, Vision, and Values

You'll recall that in Section 1, we spent a good deal of time talking about mission, vision and values. Once the new hire has acclimatized a little, then they'll be ready to absorb some of the bigger guiding frameworks that align them with the bigger picture.

Don't forget to share the mission, vision and values.

Clifton and Harter note in *It's The Manager* that there are five essential questions a new hire will wonder about during onboarding,

"1. What do we believe in around here?

2. What are my strengths?

3. What is my role?

4. Who are my partners?

5. What does my future here look like?" [30]

The answer to that first question is found in the mission, vision, and values statements. Remember it's not enough to hand them a printed copy and walk off. You need to explain why the mission, vision, and values are important to you personally, and explain how they relate to the person's particular work. As always, aim for a conversation rather than delivering an eloquent lecture.

Here's a perspective from BambooHR screenwriter and author Bryson Kearl:

> An employee's first few days on the job should be spent learning about their company and job and integrating into each. A big part of doing both is…[learning the] culture and setting clear expectations…teach new hires the definition and reasoning behind your organization's mission…vision… values and provide real-life examples of how values are applied on a daily basis…teach new hires the attitude and behaviors that are encouraged and discouraged in your workplace… tell the story or your organization and discuss… successes and failures, and the lessons learned from each… [31]

Sharing Is Caring

Never assume that your new hire knows what you think or feel about them and the value they add to your team.

Remember, sharing is caring. A best practice would be to write down a list of five things that attracted you to your new team member for their new role. Focus on soft skills that fall outside of niche skills and expertise such as:

- quick wit,
- sharp thinking on their feet, and
- calm demeanor.

Help your new team member understand what they bring to your team, so they can leverage those strengths confidently in their new role.

Be Approachable

On a scale of 1 to 10, how scary are you? If you were a shy new hire, would you be comfortable asking a difficult question? You probably don't think you are very scary at all, given that you are a wonderful person. However, what matters is how others perceive you. So here's a simple action--and you

Check in regularly on new hires. Make sure they know you genuinely want to hear their questions.

can do it right now---step out of your office and ask one of your employees whose judgement you trust (let's say it's Marjorie). "Hey Marjorie, the book here says I need to ask you something. On a scale of 1 to 10 how much do I scare new hires?"

There's your answer.

If the number is 7 or higher, then you should find a way to make yourself more approachable. Here's what you do.

"Hey Marjorie! How can I be more approachable?"

Take her advice. That should do it.

Work Twice as Hard If They're Twice as Far

If your new hire is working out of the office or part-time, then you'll have to work a bit harder to make them feel a part of the team. Here are a few tips:

- Insist on as many face-to-face meetings as is practical in the first couple of weeks. There will be things you can do remotely, but at the start there should be strong preference for face-to-face.

- When you can't do face-to-face, do a video call.

- When you can't do a video call, then pick up the phone and have a conversation.

- When all else fails, send an email.

Remember to seek conversations where you listen to the new employee. That's how you get to know them and reveal any potential questions or concerns they might have.

Staying Complaint

New hires will need to take courses on sexual harassment, safety and possibly other matters. This should be scheduled into the orientation program. It's likely HR or a compliance function in your organization will make sure this happens, however you should check that all required training is planned and actually happens.

It's not unique to new hires, but remember that employees' private information is....what's the technical word we're looking for? Oh yeah, PRIVATE. Be careful with confidential information even if in your own mind you don't think it's sensitive.

Also you may need to make accommodations if the new hire is disabled; for example if they are in a wheelchair then they need to be able to access their workplace without going up stairs. There is a whole piece of legislation called the Americans with Disabilities Act (ADA) that covers the details. Feel free to read it, but most managers would rather just call up their good friends in HR for advice on what they must do.

Compliance Do's and Don'ts

- Do make sure to make all necessary accommodations for people with disabilities.
- Do make sure all legally required training is given.
- Don't share private information about the new hire.

Back to the Story

When Maria's team lead got back from vacation, she had a pile of emails and a long list of things to do. However, the very first thing she did was check in with the new human being who had joined the team: Maria. She didn't just cruise by Maria's cubicle and wave; she invited her out for a coffee to have a good chat about how the first week had gone and how she was fitting in.

The team lead quickly recognized that Maria was adrift. She immediately booked another meeting with Maria first thing the next morning. The last thing the team lead wanted was Maria giving up and looking elsewhere for a better job. One more thing, the team lead walked into the manager's office and insisted he move around appointments so that he too could spend an hour with Maria.

You know what? That's all it took. A quick meeting with the team lead and with the manager got Maria pointed in the right direction doing useful work and feeling like a needed part of the team. That wasn't the end of the onboarding, but by prioritizing the "rescue," the team lead made sure Maria would still be there for her 30, 60 and 90 day check-ins.

Summing Up

Orientation and onboarding are simple but crucial processes for improving productivity and retention.

Here are some key points to remember:

- Delivering these processes is a partnership between HR and the manager.
- Orientation deals with the mechanics (making sure they have a desk).
- Onboarding deals with socialization and getting them to be productive.
- A few simple activities will go a long way to integrating the person into the team and making them feel welcome.
- One of the most important things is your direct involvement; show you care and be approachable.

Now, it's time for an activity.

108

HR Fundamentals for Non-HR Managers: Can We Be Friends? (& CYA!)

Can-do in Kanban: Build a Better Onboarding Process Activity

Complete the following activity with your team. Circle up with your team, then:

1. Invite each team member to recount the three best things that happened as a part of their onboarding process at your company and on your team.

2. Then, have each team member recount the three worst things that happened as a part of their onboarding experience at your company and on your team.

3. Encourage each team member to suggest actions that could improve the onboarding experience at your company and on your team.

4. Write each experience or suggestion on a sticky note. Color code the stickies, using pink for negative experiences, green for positive, and yellow for new suggestions.

5. When you are done, create a Kanban style poster board with the following "Keep, Start, and Stop" categories:

   • Keep Doing This
   • Start Doing That
   • Stop Doing That

6. Paste each positive onboarding experience (green stickies) your team members have shared in the Keep Doing This category on the poster board

7. Paste each negative experience (pink stickies) under the Stop Doing That category.

8. Paste each suggestion for ways to improve the onboarding experience at your company and on your team in the Start Doing That category (using the yellow sticky notes).

9. Then, look at the completed board and discuss with your team how you can incorporate the "Start Doing That" ideas into your existing, evolving onboarding process.

Kanban Poster Board

Keep Doing This	Start Doing That	Stop Doing That

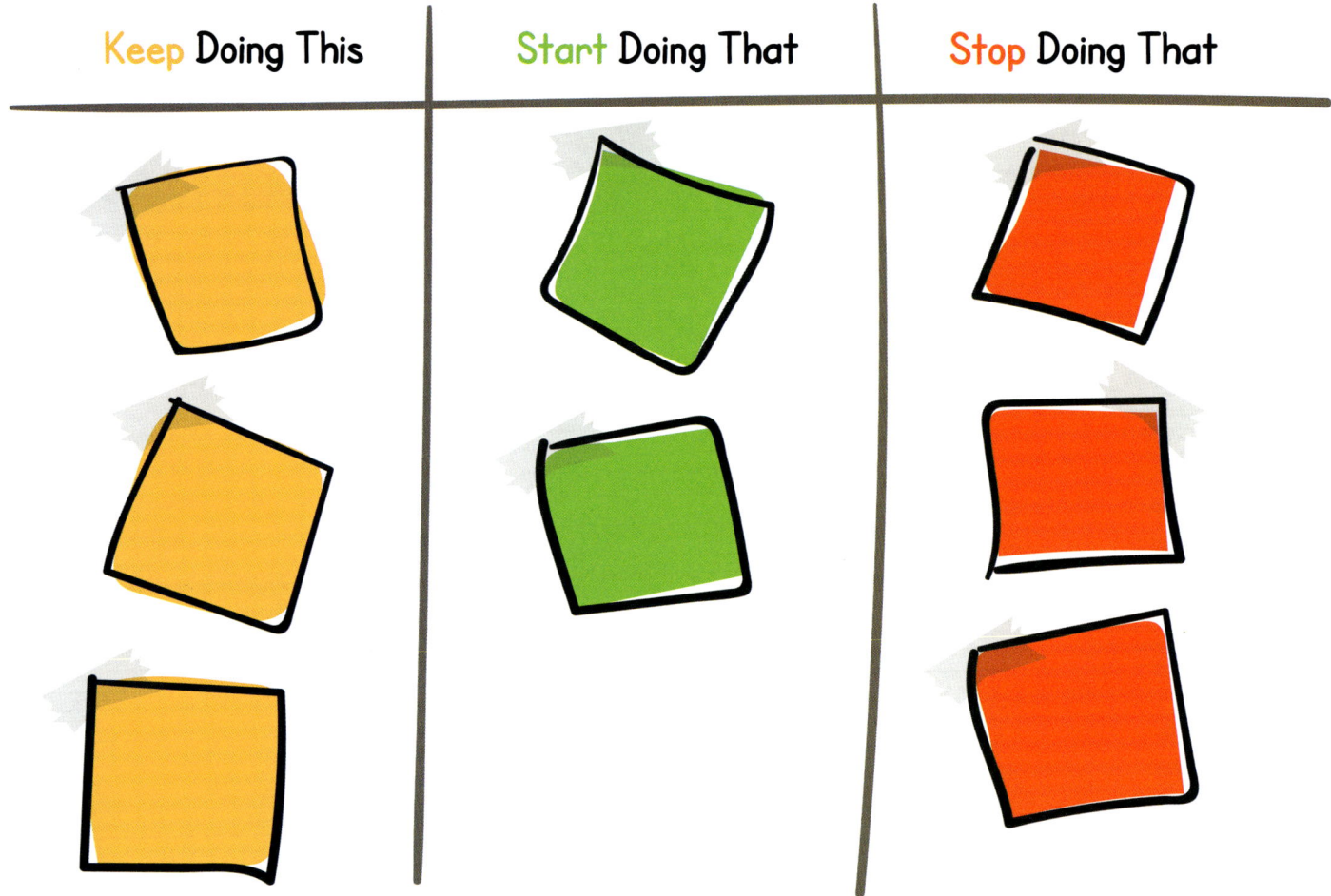

EQUIP AND ENGAGE

ONBOARDING TO DRIVE PRODUCTIVITY

Key Terms and Definitions

Productivity – the rate at which a person does useful work

Time to Productivity – how long it takes for a new employee to become competent in their job

The Issue

When a new employee starts you want them to feel welcomed, you want them to make friends, you want all documentation completed, you want them to be inspired by the mission, vision, and values—okay, enough already, now you want them to get to work.

Much of the first few days of orientation and onboarding are just getting the employee settled, now we will look at getting them productive whether they are in the office or a virtual/remote setting.

Your goal is to minimize the time to productivity, you want them fully productive and contributing as soon as possible.

A Short Story

Baruch has an exciting first week at his new job as a marketing executive. Everyone was so nice and everything had been so well organized. Now in his second week, he was hard at work responding to his boss's request to sketch out a few ideas about improving their online presence in South East Asia. He contacted various agencies specializing in the region and began to develop the project plan using a software tool he had used at his last firm. He'd even had a video meeting with the regional head--oops, he wasn't supposed to do that.

> **Onboarding isn't just about making the new hire feel welcome, it's about getting them up to speed.**

On the Friday of the second week, his boss came storming in and asked, "What the heck are you doing?" (or words to similar effect!) The Chief Marketing Officer (CMO) had received a call from the Managing Director in Singapore asking why this pointless new social media program was being launched in his region. The CMO could only mutter that she wasn't sure what was going on (in her own department) and promised to call back. Soon Baruch's boss was in the hot seat.

In Baruch's office, his boss shouted, "I asked you to *sketch out* some ideas. You don't have the authority to contact agencies, and you should never call a Managing Director. What got into your head?"

The truth was that nothing had gotten into his head because his manager hadn't put anything in there beyond a vague instruction that Baruch misinterpreted. He wanted to impress his boss by going above and beyond, and now he was in a big mess.

Hold Up for a Second - Put your Foot on the Brake

Before we go any further, we promised in the previous chapter that we would speak to the fact that some employees are not based in the office, and so the idea of popping in for a 15-minute chat or introducing them at an office meeting may not be practical.

The fact that they are out on the road, at a remote location, or working from home does not diminish their need for onboarding. It probably increases it. You still need to get them up to speed.

Here's what we think. With today's digital communications, you can figure out a way to deliver the onboarding steps listed here even if they are flying around the world on an ever-changing schedule. You can communicate by text and email. You can pre-record video messages. You can find time for voice calls, and you should insist on ensuring new employees are able to participate in video calls.

Partner with HR (and CYA)

> HR is happy to help with training but it's up to you to have a plan for bringing the new hire up-to-speed.

112

HR Fundamentals for Non-HR Managers: Can We Be Friends? (& CYA!)

Look, every situation is different so we can't prescribe what will work in your case. We are confident that you can figure something out that is practical and that achieves your onboarding goals. As you read the steps below, if they don't fit your circumstances, don't ignore them; adapt them.

As Senior BambooHR Copywriter and Author Rob de Luca noted in his article, *Creative Ways to Keep Remote Employees Engaged,*

> It might be impossible to exactly duplicate the community of an office environment for remote employees, but that's no reason not to try.

> On top of effective and constant communication, it's important to ensure remote workers interact in more ways and with more people than just the people they work with directly. [32]

Starting with Clear Objectives

How do you, as a manager, know what to do and how to get it done? Some of it is driven by processes like the annual performance management cycle. A lot of it is...well, *you just know*. You know because you've been there a while, and you know how things work. Given that your new hire hasn't been there a while, it's safe to assume that they have little idea about what to do or how to do it. It's *your* job as a manager to get them past that as soon as possible.

Think about how your organization sets objectives. Is it SMART goals, Objectives and Key Results (OKRs), Key Performance Indicators (KPIs), or something else? Whatever your organization's approach is, sit down and explain it to your new employee. Then make sure they have clarity about what they need to do, roughly how long you think it will take, and what the expected output should be. Let them know how they will be measured.

You will want to over-communicate. They need clarity from you so that they can quickly begin doing useful work. They will evolve from there into a truly productive employee who is working on the right things.

> Short but frequent check-in meetings will get the new hire up to speed quickly.

Here's how those meetings might go:

> You: "How's it going?"
>
> New employee: "Fine."

Okay, that was good right? It didn't even take 5 minutes. What did you learn? Probably nothing at all.

Instead, use the following conversation starters:

> Can you show me what you have so far?

> What could make this go faster?
>
> Explain to me what you plan to do next.
>
> Is there anything you need from me?
>
> Is there anything else on your mind?

Remember you are paying this person good money so that your team is more effective. You need to invest a little time, or they will take longer than they should to ramp up. The sooner you get them ramped up, the sooner you can leave them to their own devices.

Meet Frequently

How are your days generally? Lots of free time? I guess not. That means you don't have time to have long meetings with each new employee to give them direction and ensure they are on track. What you *can* do is have frequent, short meetings. Short means 10-15 minutes. Frequent probably means at least a couple of times a week, maybe daily in the first week or two.

> Most employees do NOT feel fully onboarded after three months. You can do better.

114

HR Fundamentals for Non-HR Managers: Can We Be Friends? (& CYA!)

Yes, This Is Worth Taking Seriously

Here's a fun fact: only 20% of new hires feel that they have been fully onboarded after their first three months on the job. As Myhre notes,

> When 20% of your people don't think they are fully on-boarded after three months...ask whether that is before or after 28% quit in the first 90 days? It's a mess either way...onboarding must be taken seriously and done right if you want to keep talented workers in the building. [33]

In the end, you can save yourself effort by putting in some effort upfront.

Here's a Different Way to Assign Tasks

Dr. Wanda Wallace, author of *You Can't Know It All* says you can delegate by asking instead of telling. She says, instead of telling an employee exactly how they should go about doing something, try giving them an objective and then asking key questions.

> "...think of delegating as a form of gentle inquiry—a process of asking questions to guide the person handling the task as he or she thinks it through. You can adjust the depth of inquiry on the basis of circumstances.
>
> What am I talking about? Suppose you have a direct report who is technically very skilled but is not thinking about the politics of the situation or about how to bring other stakeholders along in completing a project. Here's an example of delegation as inquiry.

MANAGER: Humor me by talking me through how you think this project should be approached. What are the most important things to focus on?

DIRECT REPORT: There are three issues we have to resolve technically.

MANAGER: What about stakeholders—how important are they to success?

DIRECT REPORT: They have to agree with the conclusion, or it won't get implemented.

MANAGER: OK. Let's talk about the time line. What is the final delivery date?

DIRECT REPORT: The first sign-off is in two months.

MANAGER: Working backwards from that date, who needs to sign off on this?

DIRECT REPORT: I suppose your boss needs to approve it before it goes forward.

MANAGER: Definitely! Who else will be impacted...?" [34]

Dr. Wallace points out that you can go into as much depth as needed based on the circumstances. Her approach is a fabulous way for you to figure out what they know, to help the person learn, and to leave them fully committed to the next steps.

Here's Another Idea; Explain your KPIs

New employees can't read your mind when it comes to knowing your expectations as far as their tasks, goals, and KPIs. It would help them to know, for example, that you are mightily judged on your ability to stick to a pre-ordained operating budget, and anything that they can do to help with that will be much appreciated? This may help them understand why you hesitate to buy them the latest ergonomic workstation designed by artists in Berlin. It may also lead them to point out expenses they know could be cut (like an unused subscription to a data service). Wouldn't that make your day?

Think of this as a kind of midway point between the high-level organization mission and vision and their own specific tasks.

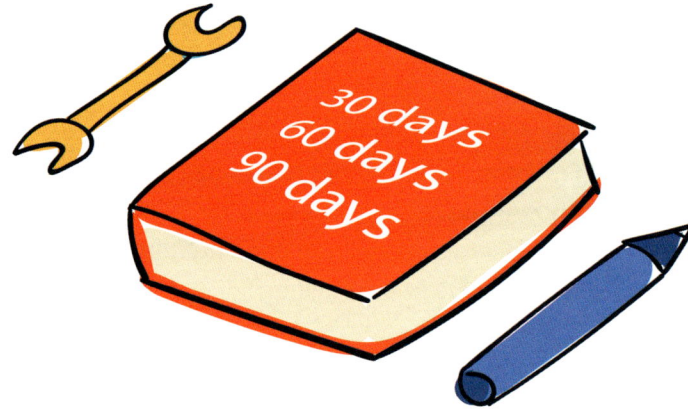

Planning for 30, 60 and 90 Days (not to be confused with *meeting* at 30, 60 & 90 days)

Sometime after the first week, it's a good idea to stretch the new employee's brain a bit by helping them come up with a plan for 30, 60, and 90 days. If it's a more senior role, that might extend to a full annual plan.

This plan can include:

- Training they need to complete
- Activities they need to achieve (e.g. meet a certain number of clients)
- Project milestones they need to complete (e.g. get the first phase of the new software tested)
- Skills they should learn (e.g. master the project management software)

The main thing you are trying to accomplish here is to get the new employee to look up and get a sense of where they are going. Don't worry too much about nailing down the perfect plan; it's just a good idea to have them aiming at something a few months out.

116

HR Fundamentals for Non-HR Managers: Can We Be Friends? (& CYA!)

The Onboarding Training Plan

Training--or more generally 'learning'– is a never-ending process. It's so important that we've devoted a whole section to it (Section 6). Training is especially important in the first few weeks or months. There are three categories of training you need to build into your onboarding training plan:

- Legally required training (e.g. if you want someone to drive a forklift, they need a licence)

- Compliance training (e.g. training about safety, ethics, and harassment so that the employees don't violate company policy or laws)

- Skills training (e.g. how to use the project management software)

Make sure you have actually created a schedule for all the training the new hire needs, and follow up to ensure it's been done.

Meeting (After Planning) at 30, 60 & 90 Days

Quite apart from planning for the next few months, an important part of onboarding is the sequence of 30, 60 and 90-day meetings that are longer and more formal than the frequent 15-minute check-ins.

You'll want these meetings to be 30 - 45 minutes in a place where you can have a relaxed conversation and where you won't be disturbed. (Smart managers know where they can hide from their own boss, peers, and employees!)

Have a formal sit-down with new hires at 30, 60 and 90 days.

Here are the sorts of things you might discuss.

30 Days (includes a compensation discussion)

– What they've learned

- What have you learned so far?
- How they are doing
- Here's where I think you are doing well
- Here's where I think you are falling short

– What their challenges are

- Who on the team are you finding helpful?
- Who is more difficult to work with?
- What tasks do you find difficult?

- How you can support them

  - What can I do to make you more effective?

- If they are getting involved with people in the company

  - Are you involved in any of the company's volunteer efforts?

  - Do you participate in any of the company's social activities?

- How the compensation system works
(or another business topic)

  - Review how they get paid, how merit increases and bonuses are decided etc.

60 Days (includes a performance management discussion)

- What they've accomplished

  - What have you accomplished so far?

- How they think they are doing

  - What do you think you are doing well?

  - Where do you think you are falling short?

- What their challenges will be

  - What do you think the big challenges will be in the next month or two?

- What resources they need

  - Is there anything you need to be more effective?

- How the performance management system works
(or another business topic)

  - Review when goals are set, how targets are decided, how results are measured, when this all happens.

90 Days (includes a career planning discussion)

- What they plan to accomplish

  - Looking ahead, what do you hope to achieve this year?

- Check-in on how they think they are doing

  - We've talked before about where you are succeeding and where you are falling short; let's revisit that.

- What their career might look like (or another business topic)

  - What are your short-term aspirations?

  - What are your longer-term aspirations?

  - Here is how job progression works at this organization."

DigitalHR notes in their article, *How Career Pathing Can Help You Win Talent and Boost Engagement*,

...21st-century employees expect more from their employer than a satisfying paycheck. They want the opportunity to grow both personally and professionally. Now, more than ever before, learning and development have become a key benefit for employees...By making their own career pathing plan employees get valuable insights... [35]

Wow, We Almost Forgot that the New Employee is a Human

Geez, we've been doing such a great job of bringing the new hire up to full productivity that we kinda overlooked the fact that they're probably a human being too. Do they have a family? Do they have pets? What do they do on the weekends? Do they have a long commute? All this human stuff is stuff that you as a boss should know.

You don't want to pry; people might want to keep their work and home life separate. Don't ask women if they are planning to have kids! However, generally, employees appreciate it when you show an interest in them as a person. It also helps you connect to them and to build a stronger, more trusting relationship. You'll learn something about what motivates them, and they may also share something about their situation that is helpful (e.g. they have a special needs child and so on, or they can't come to work on the weekend to help you prepare the budget).

There's nothing wrong with being a tough manager but you can also be the kind of boss who knows the name of an employee's cat. Being human-focused and being business-focused are not two opposing forces; they can work together.

The Magic of Checklists and Calendars

This chapter was full of suggestions on things you should do to successfully onboard an employee, so that they quickly become productive. How do you make sure that happens? The magic here isn't so magical. Sit down with your calendar and schedule these meetings. Certainly, schedule in the 30, 60 and 90-day meetings and probably schedule some weekly check-ins.

Make yourself a checklist of the things you want to talk about in your frequent check-ins, as well as in those more formal meetings. Don't lose the checklist. Refer to it. It will help you keep onboarding on track and if the onboarding is on track, then productivity will be on track.

Back to the Story

Baruch was in a mess and that's because his manager had inadvertently put him in a mess. His manager hadn't realized that—even though Baruch was a bright guy—he needed some onboarding. Luckily the manager was savvy enough to see his mistake. Baruch had been exercising initiative, and had quickly grasped the bigger picture. Those are great attributes!

The manager sat Baruch down and rather than blast him, she apologized. She said she'd been distracted with other tasks when she should have been making sure he got off to a good start. She arranged a series of check-ins and a list of topics to be covered in those check-ins so that Baruch's strengths could be aimed in the right direction.

Summing Up

Here are some key ideas to remember:

- Onboarding is not a one- or two-day process. It should include check-ins at 30, 60 and 90 days. There are many things you can do over that time to make sure that your new employee is successful.

- Don't let the length of time (up to 90 days) or the number of possible onboarding activities fool you. This is not a burdensome process. Ten minutes here and thirty minutes there is usually all it takes. It's a really smart investment of your time and will pay off many times over.

Onboarding is not a one- or two-day process.

- Clarity about objectives, KPIs, and so on is a key to getting people to full productivity as quickly as possible.

- You need frequent short check-ins or you won't know if your new employee is on-track.

- Use checklists and pre-scheduled meetings to ensure onboarding is not overlooked.

Now let's practice these ideas in an activity.

"Build-A-Bear": Equip and Engage to Deliver World-Class Onboarding Activity

Build-A-Bear studios allow people to select the components and clothes they want in order to create personalized, stuffed toys. Knowledgeable staff are available onsite to guide customers through the personalization process. Customers can select a "furry friend," and then choose the accessories, sounds, and scents they desire. Once the desired options have been selected, the toy is sewn closed and dressed so the customer can then leave with their new friend. Customers can return any time to have their toy professionally re-examined to then make subsequent changes.

For this activity, think back to your own onboarding process in your current company, and in previous companies.

- Were the people who provided you with guidance knowledgeable?

- Did they help you to implement the available tools?

- Were there any opportunities to personalize your career path?

- Were you able to revisit any of the onboarding steps you took and/or solidify any gaps?

After you've reflected on your own experience, discuss the onboarding process with your team. Have them reflect on how well they were equipped and engaged. Then, collaborate with them to consider how to use the "build-a-bear" analogy to build a more effective onboarding process! To do this, have your team create two lists from the chart below. Then, select the components from each list that you want to keep to build a better onboarding experience. Remember, you can revisit the list at any time to add, remove, or change the components, just like Build-A-Bear!

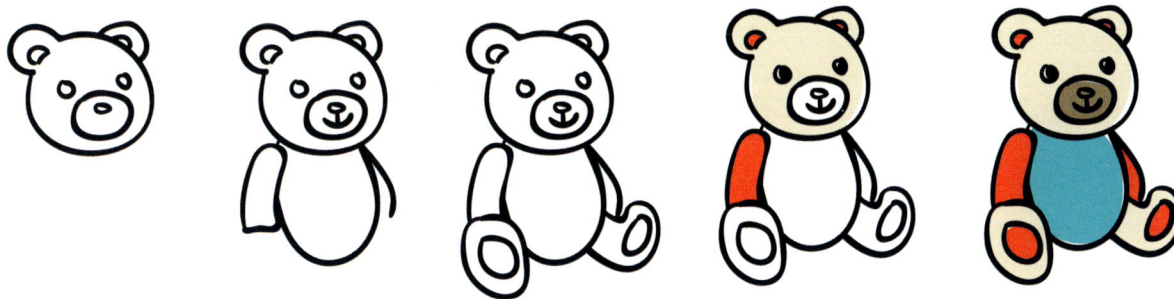

List 1: What Made You Feel		List 2: What Made You Feel	
Bored		Eager	
Uncomfortable		Inspired	
Anxious		Excited	
Worried		Anticipatory	
Concerned		Hopeful	
Perplexed		Confident	
Irritated		Motivated	

Use this activity to discover the strengths and weaknesses in your onboarding process. Enhance what has been "going well," shore up things that are identified as weak, and eliminate those that are counterproductive to equipping and engaging new hires on your team.

SECTION 5

Pay Day and the Safe Workplace:
Handling compensation, safety,
and security

SHOW ME THE MONEY

...AND THE BENEFITS

Key Terms and Definitions

Total Reward: All the elements that attract, retain and motivate employees starting with base salary right through to intangibles like learning opportunities.

Variable Pay: Bonuses, incentives or commissions that vary depending on individual and/or organizational performance.

The Issue

In this chapter, we'll sit right back and discuss compensation and benefits. Let's start by estimating how many people on your team care a lot about what's in their paycheck. (We guessed 100%. Were we right?)

Now ask: How important are benefits to them? How important are perks?

What about the people you are trying to hire? How does the compensation package affect your ability to get them to accept an offer?

Okay, we don't need to belabor this. Compensation and benefits matter a lot to people and as a manager, you need to understand how the compensation program works and be able to communicate that to your team.

A Short Story

Su Wei is the senior recruiter assigned to Lorenzo's team. The team is responsible for creating websites for companies in a variety of industries. These clients range from start-ups in financial technology (fintech) to well-established commercial construction companies in the supplies sales sector. Team members need a plethora of skill sets. For example, back-end developers need the ability to leverage Splunk on a MongoDB, and front-end developers need to be able to code in current and legacy languages (COBOL anyone?). In other words, a significant number of niche skills are required.

124

HR Fundamentals for Non-HR Managers: Can We Be Friends? (& CYA!)

Su Wei is given a checklist of all of the required and desired skills, the persona of soft skills needed, and the salary ranges for each role. An expert sourcer as well as a savvy recruiter, she begins to hunt for the rockstar-ninja-unicorn-purple squirrels needed for this team; easy peasy, right?

As she begins to engage potential candidates, she finds that she is frequently asked, "Will there be an opportunity to learn new things and experiment with new tools such as AI?" She goes back to the hiring manager to ask if he can build this into the job. He states that he wants them working 100% on today's projects, not experimenting with new tools. Su Wei continues to source for candidates and the list of viable candidates who still find the opportunity attractive dwindles. Of the scant list of remaining candidates, most were in a salary range that exceeded the target range for each respective role. Su Wei sighed. What could she do?

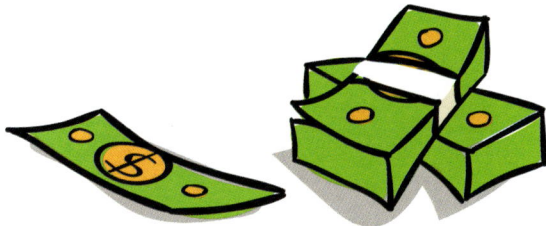

Partner with HR (and CYA)

Never say "I'd give you a raise but HR won't let me," say "If you want to know why the raise is at this level, HR will be happy to explain the process." Also, if you'd like to make an exception to the policy, talk to HR first before telling the employee what you hope to do.

Understanding Total Rewards

Long before HR became totally cool, it invented the idea of a total rewards package. It's meant to encompass all the things that create value for the employee. These elements include:

- Base salary
- Variable pay (e.g. bonuses, incentives, commission payments)
- Benefits (e.g. health care, vacation)
- Perks (e.g. free food, flexible hours)
- Working conditions (e.g. comfortable or remote workplace, fun team)
- Opportunity to learn and advance (e.g. training, interesting projects, promotion opportunities)

If you were paying close attention in Section 3 on recruiting (we know you were), you'll recall the term "Employee Value Proposition" (EVP). The total rewards package is just another way of describing the EVP.

The main point for you to remember is that even though there is a lot of emphasis on base pay, there are a whole bunch of things that make it worthwhile for a candidate to join your organization or for an existing employee to stay.

You should be super familiar with all these elements since employees and potential employees base their career decisions on these details.

How To Design a Comprehensive Compensation Program in a Complex Organization

Hah! Did that title worry you? Unless you are the head of compensation or the CHRO you won't have to worry about designing the total rewards system. In fact, you won't be given an opportunity to design one either. This means you'll have to learn to live with the one you have.

Here's one thing you really do need to know: all compensation systems have trade-offs. The total rewards at your company will *seem* to have flaws. Just remember this is a mature area of HR; these systems have been built and refined by experts; what appears as a flaw is likely just a trade-off and one that's been carefully considered by HR.

So if you don't need to design the system, what is it that you need to do? Here's the list and it's surprisingly long:

- Understand total rewards details for your company.

- Communicate about pay to your employees.

- Make sure employees know about and appreciate relevant benefits and perks.

- Explain the rationale behind the pay system.

- If you learn something relevant about reward, share it with HR.

- Get your employees' job descriptions right.

- Land a great candidate by presenting the job offer in a way that wins their heart.

Let's go through these one by one.

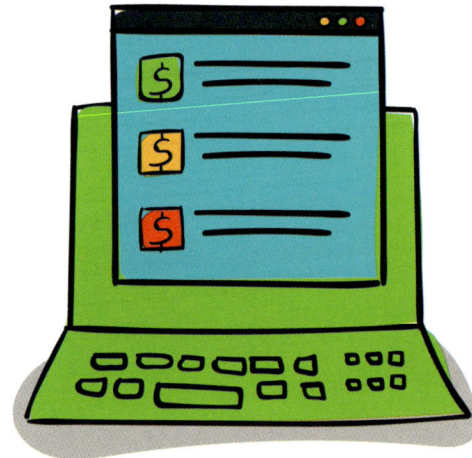

Understand How Compensation Programs Work in your Company

You can't do much about compensation and benefits if you don't understand the system, so talk to HR or other managers until you understand the mechanics. The mechanics tend to operate at two levels. There is a common-sense level where you think "Yep, that makes sense," and then there is a more arcane level that gets into the details of how it works.

Most of the time you only need to understand compensation at a common-sense level. However, sometimes you will be confronted with a situation where you do want to know the details. If you do, then you'll probably want to talk directly to the compensation specialist, and you'll want to be patient in understanding what is done and why it is done that way. As always, remember, they know a lot more about this than you; chances are your suggestions on how to do things differently have been considered and were put aside for a reason.

> **If you need to know the fine points of how the compensation system works, talk directly to a compensation specialist.**

At a common-sense level, here is how **base salary** works.

- The company comes up with a series of job grades.

- Jobs are assigned to the grades based, mainly, on how much skill and responsibility is involved. That's why a finance director ends up in a higher grade than a shipper/receiver.

- The pay level for each grade is set by looking at salary surveys that show what other companies pay for similar jobs. Usually, the pay for a grade is a range, not just one number.

- Where an individual employee sits in the pay range for their grade depends mainly on their years of experience and performance.

At a common-sense level, here is how **variable pay** works.

- The organization groups the employees into broad categories such as Executive Leadership, Managers and Professional, Hourly, and Sales (commission). Each group will have a different variable pay plan.

- The organization sets some performance metrics (e.g. for Executive Leadership one metric is likely to be profits, for a Sales Rep it's likely to be the sales made).

- A formula is created so that the higher the performance (on the metric), the bigger the bonus, incentive or commission.

- Warning: variable pay can get very complex! It's the most difficult area of total compensation and benefits.

At a common-sense level, here is how perks work.

- Perks are all over the map. In some cases, there are industry standards. For example, it might just be understood that these types of jobs get this sort of car. At other times it can be a one-off; For example, an important executive might be given a corner office.

At a common-sense level, here is how working conditions work.

- This isn't handled by the compensation department and may not even be handled by HR. The working conditions will depend on decisions made by top leadership, the facilities department, and local management.

- Wait, we missed one; *you* have an impact on the working conditions in your own unit. For example, you can probably wrangle a better coffee maker or refurbished meeting room if you try. You can also create a friendly, upbeat atmosphere that makes daily life on your team a pleasure.

Ask HR to explain anything about compensation that you don't understand

At a common-sense level, here is how opportunities to learn and advance works.

- The organization will have someone or even a whole department responsible for learning and development. They create programs and infrastructure. Individual managers have a big role in guiding that department in what learning needs their team has and in supporting employees who want to take advantage of learning opportunities.

- Career opportunities vary a lot from job to job. Sometimes the head of a function or unit, working with HR, has set up a clear progression (e.g. junior clerk to clerk to senior clerk). Other times it's ad hoc with opportunities arising and employees either directly being offered a promotion or given the chance to apply.

Communicate About Compensation to your Employees

As part of the onboarding program, you should explain to new employees, at a high level, how the system works and why they are paid what they are paid. However, even if you do a great job at this, employees will, from time to time, have questions about the compensation and benefits program. How do you handle that?

We have a big tip here. It's not common for an employee to suddenly think "Gee, I've got nothing much to do today; maybe I'll learn about the compensation program." There is usually something they are worried about or that is annoying them. They may even try to make things difficult for you by making an "innocent" comment like, "Isn't my job as important as this other job?" and from there try to make the case that they deserve a big raise.

Before diving into a direct answer about the question the employee has asked, do a little probing as to what's on their mind. Ask, "Has something happened that makes you think there's a shortcoming in the compensation system?" See where that leads.

There is often a whole other side to this that we want to touch on, which is the general coaching or performance discussions you have with employees. In these discussions, the compensation system may not come up directly, but it sits there in the background. What you want to be able to do is talk about the type of compensation that most matters to the individual. Maybe they are super motivated by variable pay – okay then talk to them about that. Maybe what they most want is some perk—hey, maybe it's even possible that you can arrange for them to get it. Maybe they want learning opportunities—that's right in your ballpark as a manager.

How do you know what motivates an individual? This is simply a big part of being a manager and you get there by getting to know your people. Talk to them. Observe them. Ask them directly. Get others' opinions on what motivates the person.

Make Sure Employees Know about and Appreciate the Relevant Benefits and Perks

It's easy to teach employees about benefits and perks, right? Just point them towards the employee handbook. Okay, here's something you gotta know as a manager: they *could* just read the handbook, but they probably won't.

> Sometimes employees don't know the benefits they are entitled to.

Why is this your concern? If an employee understands and makes good use of compensation and benefits, then they are more likely to be motivated and are more likely to stay. Sometimes employees are not aware of the compensation they are eligible for. As a manager, you do them a big favor when you clue them in. (You can also use this as an opportunity to show the employee why they should be reading the employee handbook.)

They may also simply not appreciate the dollar value of all those benefits. You don't need to pull out a spreadsheet, but you can give the employee a sense of the value and hence why they shouldn't jump ship for a small increase in base salary.

As Business News Daily noted in their article *6 Benefits That Attract Top Talent,*

> ...job seekers still care most about those bread-and-butter benefits... Employees need medical and dental insurance... but...Letting your employees work from home and providing a flexible work schedule makes their lives easier...work from home has other benefits, such as saving time and money on commuting, promoting more creativity, and encouraging a great work-life balance...casual work attire can make people feel more at ease, giving people permission to experiment and think outside the box...Offering a stipend for student loan assistance or continuing education...is an effective benefit. [36]

Explaining the Rationale Behind the Pay System

Explaining the rationale behind the organization's compensation system is something we don't see enough of. An employee comes to the manager and tells them they are underpaid (based on what they heard about what their cousin's dry cleaner's neighbor is paid). The manager tells the employee "Yes, you are right. HR is full of jerks and there is nothing I can do about it." That's unfair to HR; it's unfair to the organization, and it still leaves the employee angry. Don't do that. You want to partner with HR; it's good for you and it's good for them--which is why you don't throw them under the bus.

Instead, show the employee that you believe in the processes the organization uses, explain to them that the organization works very hard to be fair—and then tell them that you are happy to broker a conversation between them and HR so that they can learn more of the arcane details and the reasons for the trade-offs.

Employees need to know that you are willing to listen. They need to know that you'll make the effort to help them learn more. They also need to know that you truly believe that the organization genuinely does make extraordinary efforts to be fair in an incredibly complex world.

If You Know Something Relevant, Share It

If you find out that a competitor is offering an attractive compensation package in an attempt to poach your staff, then share that with your manager and HR. That doesn't mean they'll decide to match it (benefits are expensive), but they might. In any case, they will appreciate getting insights on what competitors are doing.

Get Your Employees' Job Descriptions Right

Remember in the chapter on hiring when we suggested you should actually take the time to accurately describe the job to the recruiter? Well, whenever there is a new job, or a job changes a lot, then you need an accurate description or you risk getting an inaccurate pay range. Did the job description not mention the person needed a Ph.D. in data science? No? Well, no wonder; the pay range you've been given is out of whack with reality.

Land a Great Candidate by Presenting the Job Offer in a Way that Wins their Heart

Okay, let's get to the single most potent moment when it comes to compensation offerings. It's when you are trying to land a candidate for a job and you've got to make a compelling offer. Here's how to do that.

Step one for sure is getting a sense of what they really care about. They may have some specific base salary in mind, because they need to justify the move to a significant other. They may be really driven by variable pay and will want some guarantees about how it will work. They may have limited concern about salary and benefits but are looking for chances to learn. Heck, it may be that the biggest part of your value proposition is that you'll let them work from home.

The only way you find this out is by talking to them, paying attention to the questions they ask and seeing where their eyes light up. Once you know what they care about, you have a great chance to frame the offer in a way that will win their heart.

There's also the possibility that some of the things they want are under your control. Maybe you are the one who decides how flexible to be about start and end times. Maybe you can guarantee they'll never be asked to work late on Wednesday when they have a specific childcare responsibility. Talk to them, be flexible, and find a winning deal.

As Author Jeff Haden noted in his article, *How to Make the Perfect Job Offer: 9 Tips,*

> ...Explain pay and benefits as thoroughly and accurately as possible. Describe the base salary...Then follow through with a written breakdown of all salary and benefits terms. Never give an employee any reason to feel they were the victim of a salary bait and switch—and never make...promises you cannot keep. [37]

Compliance Issues

HR will typically keep a close eye on compliance in pay. For example, you'll probably never risk paying below minimum wage because the HR systems won't allow it. The main areas of compliance you need to be concerned about are:

- Paying fairly and without bias. You can play a role in ensuring that you don't have one gender or ethnic group that is underpaid relative to another. Equal pay for work of equal value is the law, so help HR make this happen.

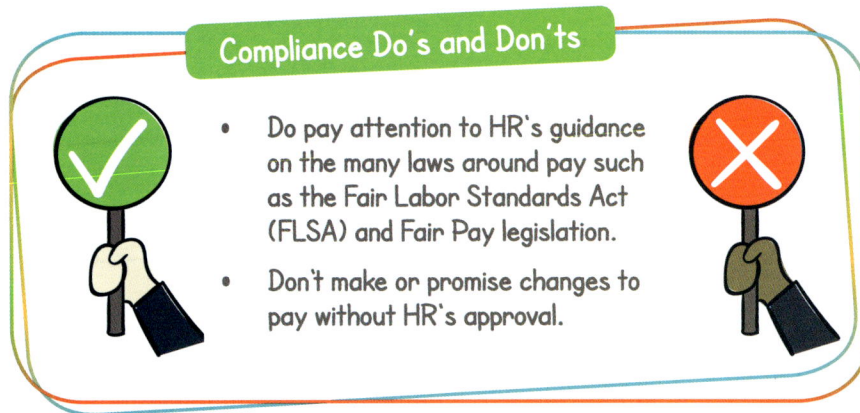

Compliance Do's and Don'ts

- Do pay attention to HR's guidance on the many laws around pay such as the Fair Labor Standards Act (FLSA) and Fair Pay legislation.

- Don't make or promise changes to pay without HR's approval.

- Using promises of a raise or bonus to get a personal favor. This means you can't suggest that an employee will likely get a raise if they help you paint your house. Yeah, we know this is obviously wrong, but it still happens sometimes. Let's be sure it doesn't happen on your watch.

Back to the Story

Eventually the recruiter, Su Wei, realized the hiring manager just wasn't tuned into the realities of hiring for this position. She marshaled her facts and asked him out to coffee. Her pitch boiled down to this: he had a choice between two profiles of candidates. One category didn't have all the skills he needed. The other category wanted excellent opportunities to expand their skill set. She'd done her job; now it was up to him to make a choice.

Lorenzo, the hiring manager, said, "Oh well, why didn't you say that before? Of course, I can build in an opportunity for them to experiment with some of the latest tools."

132

HR Fundamentals for Non-HR Managers: Can We Be Friends? (& CYA!)

> A winning job offer will appeal both to the head and the heart.

Su Wei was pretty sure she had said it before but kept politely quiet. She now was in a position to get that job filled.

Summing Up

Total rewards is the comprehensive list of offerings that HR uses to help attract, motivate and retain employees. It's another way of describing the employment value proposition (EVP).

Compensation is a complex topic, and HR works hard to make it as effective and fair as possible. Luckily, you won't have to design the system, nor will you need to know all the arcane details.

You will need to:

- Understand compensation and benefits details for your company.
- Communicate about pay to your employees.
- Make sure employees know about and appreciate relevant benefits and perks.
- Explain the rationale behind the pay system.
- If you learn something relevant about reward, share it with HR.
- Get your employees' job descriptions right.
- Land a great candidate by presenting the job offer in a way that wins their heart.

Remember, you'll get the most value from your explanation of compensation and benefits if you know the elements that matter most to each individual employee.

Now let's try an activity.

What Does your Team Really Want?

We made a big deal about knowing what individual employees want. Let's do a quick exercise where you test what you know. Make a list of employees and identify what elements of total compensation and benefits matter most to them. Be as specific as you can (e.g. rather than just say "Learning" it might be that it's going to a specific conference each year that matters a lot to them).

Team Member's Name	What Elements of Compensation They Value	How sure are you about this? (Total Guess? Kind of Sure? 100% Confident?)

SAFE AND SOUND

AVOID ACCIDENTS AND ENSURE SECURITY

You need to take the initiative in ensuring your team is safe and secure.

Key Terms and Definitions

Safety – **protections from hazards in the workplace such as those caused by equipment, facilities, disease, natural forces or human error.**

Security – **protections from humans deliberately intending harm.**

Issue

As a manager, you have an important role in implementing and enforcing your company's safety and security policies. This includes educating your employees, monitoring their behavior and enforcing compliance. You also have a duty to watch for potential hazards and see to it that danger is minimized. If you see gaps between practices, safety, and security needs, then you must ensure they are addressed.

A Short Story

Haruki was promoted to a new role in logistics that included oversight of the warehouse. He was swamped with paperwork and planning, but he did make a point of driving out to the distribution center to have a look around.

Please take all aspects of safety & security seriously. Don't cut corners. Don't allow your team to cut corners. Make sure your team has the training to be compliant, especially around harassment.

Ilya, who had been working there for approximately one hundred years, was happy to show Haruki around. Haruki was no expert on warehouses but some of the pallets seemed stacked awfully high. He also noticed some of the forklift drivers were whipping around forward and backward with what looked to him like reckless abandon. The shouts of "Ride 'em cowboy" and "Warp 9 Mr. Sulu!" added to his suspicion that they might not be taking safety all that seriously.

Haruki didn't want to look like a clueless new guy from head office, but he did manage to bring up the topic of safety.

"Ilya," he said, "how's the safety record here."

"Top notch Haruki," Ilya replied.

"Those pallets looked like they were stacked really high to me; they looked unsteady," said Haruki.

"Yep, that's how it's always been done. Gotta make the best use of the space," Ilya assured him, while sipping from the biggest cup of coffee Haruki had ever seen.

"And what about the lads on the forklifts," asked Haruki. "Do they follow the rules?"

"Oh yeah, they know I'm watching," Ilya confirmed with a laugh. "And I've got some wild stories from the old days, I'll tell you sometime."

So that was it, Haruki headed back to the world of spreadsheets in the head office. He'd asked what he thought needed to be asked and was given full reassurance by a highly experienced employee. Haruki was pretty sure things were fine; what's your opinion?

Let's Talk about Safety

Safety is about protections from hazards in the workplace such as those caused by equipment, facilities, disease, natural forces, or human error. For people working in manufacturing, distribution, or transportation, hazards are an everyday part of life. Even in offices there are health hazards especially in an era of pandemics. No one wants to see someone get hurt or sick, and most accidents are preventable. Let's think about your role as a manager in that.

136

HR Fundamentals for Non-HR Managers: Can We Be Friends? (& CYA!)

Who Is Responsible for Safety?

Organizations typically have a safety department that may report to HR, an operational leader (such as the Chief Operating Officer) or the head of Environmental Health and Safety. This individual or department is the key figure in defining the policies, processes, training and data collection needed to ensure worker safety.

Other parts of the organization will collaborate with the safety professionals including legal, HR and the operational managers (e.g. plant manager, warehouse manager). There are also external bodies such as government inspection agencies, the companies you supply, and industry associations that might have an interest in safety. Finally, particularly in non-office environments, it is understood that each worker has a critical role to play in keeping themselves and their co-workers safe day-to-day.

Phew, that's a relief, isn't it? With so many smart people involved in safety, presumably, you are off the hook. Maybe you can skip this section and spend some time answering emails – okay, not so fast. As a manager, you have an important responsibility to keep your employees safe.

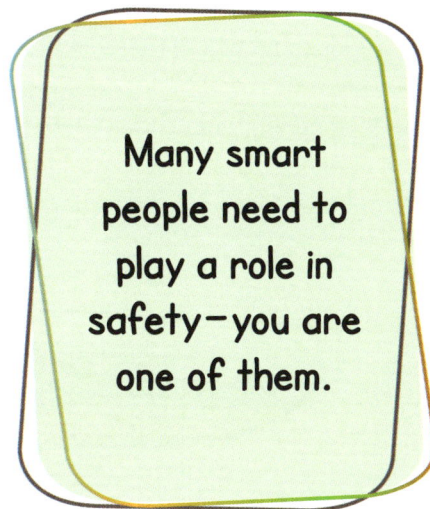

> Many smart people need to play a role in safety—you are one of them.

A Manager's Role in Safety

Let's start with the most important thing you need to do in keeping your employees safe: keep your eyes and ears open. Many hazards are clearly visible if you make the effort to look for them. Is there something on the floor that someone will trip over? Are vehicles zooming around when people are walking by? Is someone trying to lift a heavy object by themselves? If you are alert to safety hazards, just as a responsible adult, then you can make sure they are dealt with.

Well, that takes care of eyes; what about ears? This simply means listening to your employees if they suggest something might be a danger. Take the time to talk to them about possible dangers. It's all about alertness and paying attention.

Now there are also some more formal responsibilities:

1 Know the rules. You need to know the safety rules of your organization. Your safety professional will be happy to tell you what they are, and there should also be safety documentation. Ask for it. Read it. Then make sure the rules are being followed.

2 Education and training. You don't need to give training, but you do need to be sure it is being given. You should also care enough about your team's well-being that you'll check that the quality of the training is up to par. Sit in on a session. Ask employees how they will use the training they just completed. Ask them to what degree their learning will help them do their work. Make sure they understand it.

3 Submit any necessary reports and keep any necessary documentation. You may need to submit reports and keep documentation related to safety such as an accident report. Do you know what is required in your organization? Not sure, then ask your safety department.

4 Enforce the rules. Did we mention that it's not enough to know the rules? Ensure employees know the rules and make sure they are being followed. We did cover it in point 1, but let's mention it again. It's rarely the case that accidents occur because there wasn't a rule. It's usually because someone didn't follow the rule. Your job is to make sure they do, even if it seems like overkill.

5 Build a safety culture. If you are in an organization where there are serious hazards (i.e. a factory not an accounting consultancy), then there is a good chance HR will be promoting a safety culture. Take your lead from them on how to make safety a top of mind concern every day.

6 Identify safety gaps. Look for dangers and collaborate with the safety professionals to close any safety gaps.

Common Safety Hazards

Take a moment to think about some of the safety hazards that exist in your organization. Think department by department, location by location, maybe job by job. What sort of things come to mind? How long is the list?

Safety hazards depend very much on the type of operation you are running. A nail salon has different risks from a nuclear power plant, which has different risks from an airline. Nevertheless, let's share a few common hazards:

> **Slips and falls are a common cause of on-the-job injuries.**

- Slip, trip, and fall hazards
- Dangerous chemicals
- Moving equipment
- Lifting heavy objects
- Ergonomic hazards (e.g. repetitive strain injuries)
- Extreme temperatures
- High stress (e.g. air traffic control)

Harassment

There is a whole other category of safety issues that deals with emotional well-being rather than physical well-being. These issues revolve around employees being subject to bullying, scapegoating, belittling, and sexual harassment. We will group these all under the general heading of "harassment." Harassment typically falls in the realm of HR and may not be covered by a safety officer.

There are two main types of situations: peer to peer harassment and boss to subordinate harassment. Boss to subordination harassment is particularly serious because of the power differential. If you are a manager of managers then you must keep your antenna tuned for boss to subordinate harassment and deal with it swiftly and sternly. If the harassment is sexual or bigoted, then you need to involve HR right away. If the harassment is serious, you need to involve HR right away. If the harassment goes on after you've told a manager to "cut it out, now," then you need to involve HR. The message is pretty clear. Boss to subordinate harassment is a serious matter, and it's the kind of thing that can get a manager fired, damage the organization's reputation, and damage your reputation as well.

Peer to peer harassment is a bit trickier for you to handle because it varies from friendly ribbing, which everyone enjoys, to subtle put-downs that leave an employee feeling bad, to reallly inappropriate behavior. It's all too easy to classify all but the worst behavior as "friendly ribbing," because then you don't have to deal with it. (Don't go this all too easy route!)

> **Managers have a legal and moral responsibility to get tough on harassment.**

Remember too that the bully may be behaving badly because other people are not being cooperative. If purchasing is taking its sweet time to fill an order that an employee desperately needs, then that employee may resort to yelling. Some people genuinely are mean, some people are overly eager to take offense, and often it's a mix of things; so make sure you get the full story before assuming the person accused of bullying is totally in the wrong.

Here's some advice:

- With sexual or bigoted harassment you can easily run afoul of the law. Don't tolerate this even if "it's all in fun." Explain to employees that there are legal risks, and you need them to behave professionally on the job.

- Don't assume that when someone says "It's okay, I don't mind," that that makes it okay. No one likes to rat on their teammates. You need to be sensitive to the underlying vibe, not just what your employees are willing to say.

- Do a little asking around to get the full picture before concluding who is in the right and who is in the wrong.

- Intervene before things get out of hand. Friendly ribbing can evolve into unfriendly ribbing and from there to outright harassment. Don't let things escalate. Set standards for professional behavior and enforce them.

> Don't tolerate this even if "it's all in fun."

Generally, you don't need to be heavy handed about this. Often it's enough for you as the boss to tell people "You gotta cut that out. Maybe you can do it at home but you can't do it here." If that doesn't work, call the perpetrator in for a one-on-one and lay down the law. Make it clear that it is you enforcing a code of conduct, not you reacting to someone complaining. Sometimes, if the harassment doesn't stop, you'll need to terminate the employee. As always, when in doubt, call HR.

Risk Factors

So why are there still accidents when many organizations are pretty savvy about risk, the people have been trained, and you're doing your best to keep an eye on things? Here are some of the things that increase the risk of accident:

Newbies

The Bureau of Labor Statistics notes that,

"...nearly 40% of injured workers have been on the job less than a year. New workers are more likely to be hurt because they lack the experience and information needed to properly protect themselves on the job..." [34]

You may want to read that statistic again: 40%! You gotta protect the newcomers. They don't know what they don't know.

The Old Guard

Just for fun, go talk to some of the older workers about how safety was handled "back in the day." In the past, safety standards were much laxer. Ask your grandparents about old attitudes to drinking and driving. Heck, ask them about the seatbelts in their first car! ("Seatbelts? Never did see a need for those new-fangled things!") What you as a manager have to watch out for are members of the old guard who still prefer to do things the old way. Check

that they know the new rules, that they know why there are new rules, and check that they adhere to them.

Fatigue

Fatigue increases the likelihood of an accident.

"According to the National Highway Traffic Safety Administration, every year about 100,000 police-reported crashes involve drowsy driving. These crashes result in more than 1,550 fatalities and 71,000 injuries. The real number may be much higher, however, as it is difficult to determine whether a driver was drowsy at the time of a crash." [35]

If you have shift workers, people who work long hours, people who have a second job (and let's not forget people with infants), then fatigue is a risk you need to watch out for.

Hurry, Pressure, Stress

Okay, this is where we get to the stuff that really might be your fault. When people are rushed, they are more likely to bend safety guidelines or simply

make a mistake. If you are rushing people too much, you are putting them at risk. Don't do it.

High-Reliability Organizations & Safety Culture

Do you work in the emergency room of a hospital, on the flight deck of an aircraft carrier, as a forest firefighter or in a nuclear reactor? If so, you'll be interested to know that many of these organizations where high risk is an hour by hour reality have developed what is called a "high-reliability organization" with an intense safety culture.

Stress is a hazard in itself as well as being a cause of accidents.

> Dangerous places, like the flight deck of an aircraft carrier, can be made much safer with the right culture.

High-reliability organizations expect the unexpected. In *Managing the Unexpected: Resilient Performance in an Age of Uncertainty,* Karl Weick and Kathleen Sutcliffe write:

> "...organizations that persistently have less than their fair share of accidents seem to be able to sense significant unexpected events than organizations that have more accidents." [40]

If you're a manager in a dangerous environment, then you'll want to go much deeper into the topic of safety than what we've covered here.

The ROI of Safety

Being safe pays off as AMTrust Financial notes in their report, the *ROI of Safety: How to Create a Long-Term Profitable Workplace Safety Program,*

> The amount of workplace injuries [in the US] has declined over the past 15 years due to improved safety conditions and requirements...the workplace has gotten safer for employees over the years...The true cost of work-related injuries is much more than just the cost of workers' compensation insurance and medical bills. It impacts the workplace both directly and indirectly. [41]

Take a gander at these direct and indirect costs. You don't need to be a financial genius to recognize the value of staying safe.

Direct Costs	Indirect Costs
Indemnity (wage replacement) payments	Workplace disruptions
Medical bills (if the company is liable)	Loss of productivity
Civil liability	Decrease in morale
Litigation costs	Worker replacement
Property loss and/or repair	Additional required training
	Increased insurance costs
	Federal/national fines and/or legal costs
	Damage to the company brand/reputation

SECURITY

Let's Talk about Security

Security is about protections from hazards caused by humans deliberately intending to cause harm. There are not many people going around deliberately causing harm, but it doesn't take many to make life miserable for us all.

As a manager who looks out for your team, you'll want to understand and support the security measures your company has in place.

Who Is Responsible for Security?

It gets a little complicated in deciding who is responsible for security. The two big buckets are:

- Physical security (e.g. fences, guards, locked doors) – that's usually handled by the facilities department

- Cybersecurity (e.g. passwords, firewalls) – that's usually handled by IT

It gets complicated by the fact that parts of physical security may be outsourced to a third-party firm (e.g. a company that supplies guards and alarm systems) and the facilities department may report into HR, CFO, VP of Administration or somewhere else.

As a manager, you really ought to know who is who in the organization. If you don't know, then find out. In fact, there's a general lesson here that as a manager you pay a lot more attention to the broader organization than you do when you are just a regular employee.

Now ask either the person in charge of physical security or cybersecurity what their biggest problem is. Is it an obscure anarchist hacker group living in a super cool warehouse in L.A? Is it a team of rogue MI5 agents who are breaking into your office place to steal purses? No, the biggest problem is that employees flout the rules (e.g. propping open a door that's meant to be secure or giving their password to a random caller who claims to be from IT).

And this brings us to the broader responsibility. Every employee has to play their part and you are responsible for ensuring your team does so.

A Manager's Role in Security

Specifically, as a manager, you should:

1 **Know the rules.** Learn what policies and procedures have been put in place by whoever in your organization takes the lead on physical security and cybersecurity. Go one better and learn *why* those policies are in place. If something doesn't make sense to you then ask.

2 **Educate.** Make sure employees know the rules. Ask them if they understand why the rules are in place, and if they don't know then tell them.

3 **Enforce.** Yeah, I know this sounds harsh. You don't want to be the cop going around berating people for bending the rules. Yet, you've got to do it. This more than anything else is how you improve security. (OK, maybe we should call it Enforce Nicely. Doesn't that sound better?)

4 **Report**. If there is a security incident, report it. This is true even if nothing bad happened. If somehow a strange person with no security badge was walking around, then you should let the person in charge of physical security know.

5 **Identify security gaps.** The heads of physical and cybersecurity can't be everywhere at once; they can't know every possible security weakness. Keep your eyes and ears open to learn about security gaps and work to close them.

Don't overlook the security issues of employees who work off-site--they are your responsibility too. Set up a call with these employees and with someone who handles security in your company to see if there are any issues you need to be aware of. If you can't arrange a call, then a security professional can help you craft a questionnaire to check for issues that may need attention.

Common Security Issues

What are the common security issues in your organization? What have you seen? What stories have you heard? It's not a bad idea to ask some old-timers what's happened over the years.

Crooks won't just steal your purse; they might steal your data.

144

HR Fundamentals for Non-HR Managers: Can We Be Friends? (& CYA!)

> **Learn the security policies and procedures in your organization.**

These are some common issues:

- Petty theft
- Vandalism
- Cybercrime
- Harassment by other employees
- Harassment by an ex-spouse or significant other
- Threats of harm, or actual harm, by a disgruntled employee or ex-employee
- Privacy breaches

Of these, it's with the last three where you play a special role. The head of security won't know that someone on your team has gone through a bad breakup with a violent boyfriend or girlfriend—but you might. You are much more likely to know if you are attuned to employees and talk to them when something seems wrong.

If you do know that a specific individual might pose a risk then ask the security guards, others on your team and people in reception to keep an eye out for them. Talk to the experts in security and HR for other tips on how to minimize the risk.

Privacy is an issue for you as a manager because you likely have confidential information about your employees that should be protected. Keep confidential information under lock and key (and sealed lips!) just like you'd keep a pile of cash protected.

Risk Factors

The biggest risk factor is simply the organization or employees not taking security risks seriously. This is where you have to lead by example. Your attitudes and actions will have a big influence on how well your team is protected.

What about Employees Who Work Remotely?

Remember that just because someone is working remotely or on the road, it doesn't mean you're not responsible for safety and security. You need to handle these situations case by case. Someone doing accounting from a home office is in a rather different situation from one who drives a big truck.

Even though each situation is unique, there is a general answer. Talk to the person so you know the situation, and talk to the safety and security professionals in your organization to see if there is something you ought to be doing.

Compliance Do's and Don'ts

- Safety and security have many serious compliance requirements. Don't ignore your responsibility to stay up-to-date in these areas.

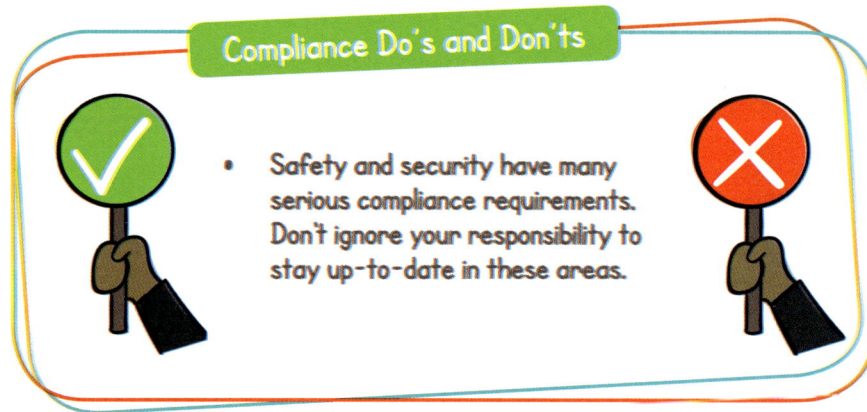

- Workplace Harassment training
- Workplace Safety training
- Workplace Violence Prevention training

Compliance Issues

Because you are a responsible human being you will want to look after the safety and security of your employees. Even an irresponsible human being will want to do so because there are compliance issues involved.

You need to work with HR and any compliance professionals in your organization to make sure you know the rules relevant in your organization. There is a pretty good chance that there will be legal or company compliance rules around providing:

- Affirmative Action training
- Americans with Disabilities Act (ADA) training
- Discrimination training
- Ethics and Code of Conduct training
- Human Rights training
- Privacy training
- Sexual Harassment training

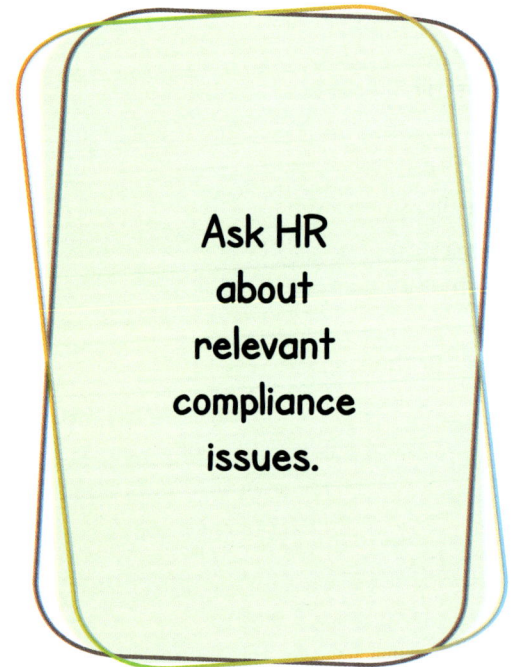

Does that sound like fun? Maybe not, but that's why you get paid the big bucks. Remember, you're not on your own in sorting this out; HR and other departments will probably be doing the heavy lifting. Your job is to be a superb collaborator.

Ask HR about relevant compliance issues.

One thing you can do to make this better for everyone is to focus on the "why." Too often compliance training is a "tick the box" exercise and everyone seems happy just to be able to say they did it. You should do a little introduction for employees explaining why these compliance rules were made in the first place and why it is important to you that the team learn them.

Back to the Story

Haruki took Ilya's word for it that everything was fine. Then a stack of boxes did fall over slightly injuring a summer intern. Haruki's explanation to his own boss, "Yep, I thought that might happen," didn't go down too well. Haruki was responsible for the warehouse, and that meant he was responsible for the safety of the people working in the warehouse. Haruki's boss let him know in no uncertain terms that this was a grave oversight and it mustn't happen again.

Summing Up

Yes, it's true that a manager has a lot of different things they need to keep an eye on, not just getting results from their team. Two of those other things are safety and security.

- Both safety and security are largely the responsibility of other parts of the organization, but you and your team have a big role to play.

- Your main role in safety and security revolves around knowing the rules, communicating the rules, and ensuring your team follows them.

Safety and security
are both a financial
issue and a
humanitarian one.

- You also play an important role in identifying any gaps that the heads of safety and security may be unaware of.

- You should be aware of safety risk factors like fatigue. If you don't keep an eye on reducing these risk factors, it can undo all the work you, your team, and the organization have put into creating a safe and secure environment.

- Safety and security are both a humanitarian duty and a financial one. Take it seriously.

The Jenga Tower: Building A Safe and Secure Workplace Activity

Have you ever played the rectangular block game, Jenga? The game provides you with wooden logs, which you must stack to build a tower. The goal is to keep putting one log atop another, and then take turns pulling them out, one at a time, without toppling the tower. Purchase a generic game set or just plain wooden playing logs at a local discount or hobby shop. Divide your team into two groups. Then:

1 Have one group compile a list of safety policies in your workplace.

2 Have the second group compile a list of security policies in your workplace.

3 Spread the logs you have purchased on a table.

4 Have each group write one of the items from their list across one side of each log.

5 When they are done, have the groups take turns stacking the logs to build a tower.

6 As each group adds a log to the tower, have team members state additional measures that could be implemented to strengthen safety and security on your team. For this step, you'll want to have team members take turns, giving each person a chance to speak.

Once the tower is built, see if taking one policy out of the stack will make it all fall to the ground. This is a great kinesthetic way to see what happens if even one policy is not adhered to.

This activity can help make your team more aware of, sensitive to, and willing to be proactive in the prevention of workplace safety and security issues. It's a great "team building" activity! (Pun intended.)

SECTION 6

Train, Coach & Inspire:
Turn raw talent into real results

TRAINING TO WIN

HOW MUCH IS A TRAINED EMPLOYEE WORTH?

Talk to HR about what makes training effective

Key Terms and Definitions

Training to improve productivity – training in skills or knowledge to help employees perform better.

Training in compliance – training so that employees know relevant regulations and policies.

Legally required training – training that is required by law for that job.

The Issue

One of the main factors affecting job performance is whether or not the employee knows how to do the job. Now that we spell that out, it seems too OBVIOUS to say, but stick with us here. An employee comes into the job already knowing how to do a lot, and there are several things they'll learn on the job on their own. However, that isn't enough to optimize performance. You'll get better performance if you invest in effective training.

We need to toss in the word "effective" because sending someone off to a course just so you can tick off the box, "Training done," is pointless. So, as the manager, your job isn't just to make sure some training is going on; your job is to keep a close enough eye on it that you can be confident that it's helping to improve performance. In fact, what you are really aiming for is a learning culture where learning is genuinely encouraged, supported, and designed to fit each employee's needs. You also want an environment where people coach each other, look up how to do things on YouTube, read articles, and take a moment to reflect on lessons learned after a project.

150

HR Fundamentals for Non-HR Managers: Can We Be Friends? (& CYA!)

There's one more important element to this: people. (Yes, in management-related matters the issue of people seems to come up often.) Most people want to learn, and many people love to learn, so providing a workplace where learning is a priority is an important part of your employee value proposition. Remember an investment in training is an investment in retaining your best workers.

A Short Story

Rajesh was having a bad day. He felt he was going to have to fire the new financial temp...that was going to be unpleasant. Then he was going to have to call up the temp agency and yell at them for sending a lousy temp...that wouldn't be fun (Rajesh is a sweet guy; he doesn't like to yell). Finally, he was going to have to tell his boss that the critical financial report he had promised to deliver was going to be late...so, let's just say the temp wasn't the only one at risk of being fired.

Here's how it started. The brand new temp Ruby had come in on time as expected. Rajesh showed her the report she needed to produce. She seemed to understand completely - which was to be 'expected' since Rajesh had insisted the temp agency send him a highly trained person. He then explained to her (not once but twice) that his report typically took the woman she was temporarily filling in for most of the day to do. He pointed out that it would likely take her longer, and she might well have to stay late. Ruby seemed okay with that too. This was looking good!

Partner with HR (and CYA)

You'll get better performance if you invest in effective training.

Then at 10:00, Rajesh had seen Ruby in the lunchroom having a coffee and chatting with one of the staff members. He strolled by at 10:30, and she was still there happily chatting away. This woman was a slacker! He was doomed.

After he composed himself, he barged into the coffee room with a fierce expression on his face. Ruby (aka "Ruby the slacker" in his mind) smiled like she'd seen an angel.

"Oh good," she said. "I've been looking for you everywhere. Here's the report. I wanted to get it to you right away so you could check it. I know how important this is."

He took the papers and checked the report. Then he checked again. There was something weird about that report. It was perfect.

"Ummm, yeah, uh," Rajesh said, trying to flip his brain from the phrase, "You're fired," to "You did a fantastic job."

Ultimately, he found the words he was looking for. "Ruby, how is it that you got this done so quickly? Normally it takes all day."

"Oh, that," Ruby explained. "It was just a few pivot tables, so it only took an hour. From what I can tell, the other worker must have been doing it manually."

Rajesh took a moment to process that. The regular worker used Excel all the time. The regular worker was diligent and experienced. However, the evidence suggested she didn't know Excel all that well. Why hadn't she learned? Why hadn't she been given a little training? Rajesh caught his reflection in the mirror. He knew who ultimately was to blame.

Three Broad Categories of Training

Our story hinted at a lack of training in a necessary skill; generally, it's useful to distinguish between three broad categories of training:

> Make sure your employees don't inadvertently break the law!

- **Training to improve productivity**. Productivity training includes things like technical skills, listening skills, and product knowledge.

- **Training in compliance**. Compliance training ensures employees know the laws and regulations relevant to their work so that they don't inadvertently break any laws. For example, there are laws about how you dispose of chemicals and how you handle personal data.

- **Legally required training**. This is training a person must have to be allowed to do the job. For example, someone will need appropriate training (and licensing) to drive a truck. There are also many jobs that require a certain amount of training every year for the individual to maintain their professional designation. The company might need to prove employees in certain jobs have had the relevant and required training (which may involve certificates or licensing).

So many compliance rules and details to keep track of! Do you ever wonder who is responsible for compliance training and legally required training in your department? Hey, this isn't something you should *wonder* about! This is something you should **know** about because there is a chance that the person responsible is you.

> You are responsible for knowing what training is required.

The larger the company, the more likely compliance and legally required training are effectively handled by HR or some other department. They will often ensure that the organization is up-to-date on the relevant regulations, that appropriate training is given, and that records are kept. In a smaller organization, the onus may be less on HR and more on you.

In an ideal world, all you needed to know about compliance would have been covered when you were onboarded to your managerial role. If it wasn't explained to you, now is the time to find out. When we say now we mean *right now*. Put down this book and send an email to HR asking for a meeting to go over all the details of the training required for each job in your department.

Learning Strategy

Once you are confident you are on top of required legal and compliance training, you can turn your mind toward training —or more generally *learning*—to improve productivity. Since this is important to your team's success, you had better have a strategy.

A strategy is built from:

- Understanding what your team needs to learn (we call this "learning needs analysis")

- Figuring out what learning programs will meet these needs

- Securing any necessary budget

- Planning how and when the learning programs will be carried out

- Following through on implementing the plan

The strategy can probably be noted down in just a few pages; it's not the length of the plan that matters, it's that you've put quality thought into creating it.

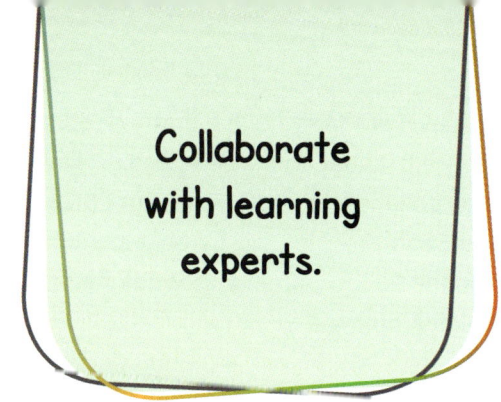

Collaborate with learning experts.

Learning Needs Analysis

Identifying the right learning programs for your team should be a collaborative process based on team needs and will depend on the training structure in your organization. The life of a manager in a company with an established Learning & Development department (call it "L&D" - it shows you're in the know) is very different from the life of a manager in a company with just one HR pro.

However, in all cases the right training for your team will depend on:

- what they do and how they do it,

- what they need to learn,

- how long they have to learn it, and

- best practices designed to enhance retention.

Section 6 • Chapter 1 • Training to Win: How much is a trained employee worth?

153

You will probably have a pretty good sense of those four points and if you collaborate with HR or your L&D function, then you will be able to clearly define learning priorities for each employee.

Finding or Developing Learning Programs

While you can take a pass at developing training yourself, if you truly want it to be successful and help drive team goals, it is highly recommended that you work with a professional: either a consultant or an expert within your own organization. This person should be someone who can help deliver the compliant, branded, engaging learning content you need. (Help is on the way!)

It should be noted that HR/Leadership may have some specific training available from their division. If you have a Learning and Development (L&D) division, you can work with them to create or buy the learning resources you desire. (Aren't you lucky?!) Smaller companies may not have an L&D division established, but will likely have someone on point who is

> Not all problems are best solved by training. Diagnose the underlying cause before you send someone to a training program.
> #HaveMoreThanJustaHammer

specifically assigned to handle training development and implementation. Work with this person to help you craft or buy meaningful learning programs for your team.

So, now your biggest task is to clearly communicate your team's needs to the point person for training. Think about what your team members need to be able to do better or more consistently.

- What (do you believe) hinders them from doing it?

- How much time can be dedicated to training?

These are critical questions to answer. You may find that there isn't a need for training at all if simply changing a work process can resolve the challenge or remove the issues preventing your team from doing their jobs better. Silver linings ahead!

Communicating clearly is also critical to ensuring that you get the end results you want. Your training professional is not a mind reader and cannot be clear on what you need unless you clarify it. Don't worry, this won't be hard. They'll ask for the information they need. You just need to make time for them. They will want you to:

- Articulate your desired end goals clearly
- Clarify how work performance should change
- Explain how you will evaluate outcomes

Remember too that your HR or L&D pro will be an expert in learning, but not in the particular topic you want to teach. You'll have to put them in touch with experts on the subject. (Maybe that's you!?)

There are amazing learning resources available in the world. If you are very clear about what you need, then your L&D specialist will be in a good position to buy, adapt, or create exactly what you need. Focus on what your team needs to change, and let your L&D specialist focus on how to get there.

Feedback Will Ensure Continuous Improvement
As learning programs are being developed or piloted you will need to provide early feedback to your learning

It's in your best interest to have a team that is continuously learning.

specialist. Your feedback will allow them to adjust course as needed before getting too far in the process. Be sure that your feedback is clear and honest! Do not agree to or create training that is off-topic or otherwise "missing the mark" on what your team must be able to learn or do.

There is a pot of gold at the end of all this work. For starters, a well-trained team will be remarkably more productive. From your team's perspective, the opportunity to learn

and grow is something they will value. Strengthening and expanding their knowledge can boost your team members towards their career goals. Learning programs will demonstrate that you care about their development, which can help create greater loyalty to the company and your team.

What is Your Responsibility for Training to Improve Productivity?
You are the individual who is most responsible for helping your employees develop their skills. Yes, HR cares a lot about this. Yes, your manager will also care. However, you know your employees better than anyone else. Furthermore, your performance depends on their performance. It is very much in your interest to have a team that is continuously learning.

You should be constantly on the lookout for any opportunity to help and encourage your employees to learn. Sometimes it is formal training, sometimes it's working with a peer, and sometimes it's direct help from you.

Section 6 • Chapter 1 • Training to Win: How much is a trained employee worth?

155

One of the most important parts of this responsibility is that you have to carve out time for employees to participate in learning programs. If you cannot make this happen, then there is no point having a learning strategy at all.

Learning Agility and the Growth Mindset

In a way, what you are trying to do with your learning strategy is to create what HR calls "learning agility." Here's how George Hallenbeck describes it in the Korn Ferry Institute white paper, *Seven Faces of Learning Agility*:

People who are Learning Agile:

- Seek out experiences to learn from,

- Enjoy complex problems and challenges associated with new experiences,

- Get more out of those experiences because they have an interest in making sense of them,

- Perform better because they incorporate new skills into their repertoire.

A person who is learning agile has more lessons, more tools, and more solutions to draw on when faced with new business challenges. [42]

You can see how this is different from just sending people to a bunch of courses. You want your employees to be enthusiastic learners. You want them to actively seek out opportunities to learn. That enthusiasm will flow from your own attitudes. If your team sees that you support learning, if you applaud people who try out new things, and if you show that you are constantly learning yourself, then you'll build a team culture that naturally has learning agility.

Important research on an attitude called "The Growth Mindset" underlies the concept of learning agility. The research is discussed in Stanford professor Carol Dweck's book *Mindset: The New Psychology of Success*. Dweck explains that some people have a "fixed mindset" when it comes to skills. They might

> Have a growth mindset; know that people can always get better.

think "I'm good at math" or "I'm bad at public speaking" and see that as a fixed trait. If it's fixed, then there is not much point in trying to get better. With a growth mindset, people believe they can always get better.

The research shows that a growth mindset leads to better results. A fixed mindset discourages people who need improvement in a skill from trying to get better ("Oh, I'm just no good giving presentations so why bother; get someone else to do it"). Strangely, it can also prevent people who excel at a skill from getting better as fast as they should. One reason this occurs is that they don't feel they need to try hard.

Compliance Do's and Don'ts

- Do take compliance training seriously.
- Don't tell employees it isn't important.

Note that the growth mindset doesn't mean everyone can be a superstar. There are innate differences in ability. However, everyone can improve, and they can improve to a surprising extent. For most of the tasks people need to do in business, you don't need to be a superstar—you just need to be competent.

Now let's bring this back to your own attitudes. Do you believe in each of your employees' potential to learn? Do you think their skill level is fixed or do you think it can get much better? If you believe in them, then it will help them believe in themselves. You'll be pleased with the results.

Back to the Story

The great thing about Rajesh as a manager was that his first instinct was to blame himself, not his employee. The regular employee didn't know what she didn't know. Neither did he. He made a point of asking the temp, Ruby (aka "Ruby the Excel genius" in his mind), to stay an extra half-day when the regular worker returned to show her a few tricks.

After that, he closed the door to his office and spent half an hour writing down the skills or topics that each of his staff members might most need to learn. He planned to then run these by the employees to see if they made sense. But now he was confident he had taken a step towards higher productivity.

Summing Up

Training is important to your HR department and it is important to your success. It's easy to overlook it in the rush to get today's work done. That's why good managers create a learning strategy and partner with HR and/or Learning & Development to implement it. Some key things to remember are:

- Some training is legally required, and some is required by your company so that employees remain compliant.

- Other training is aimed at improving productivity.

- Chances are that legally required training and compliance training will be led by HR or another department. It's your responsibility to know what is required and support the efforts to make it happen.

- Training to improve productivity is your responsibility, usually in close partnership with HR.

- It's not enough to just send employees to training programs. You need to create a mindset that embraces learning. We say that people who embrace constant learning are "learning agile" and have a "growth mindset."

Now, let's move on to an activity that will bring insight into what makes for effective training.

Section 6 • Chapter 1 • Training to Win: How much is a trained employee worth?

157

The E.T. (Effective Trainer): Building An Effective Training Approach Activity

Work through the following activity independently. Take a look at the chart below. In the Best Trainer column, list the names or initials of the top three most effective trainers or teachers whose approach to education is engaging and interactive. The trainer or teacher can be from your high school, college, or your professional experience. Think about what made the training they delivered memorable, meaningful, and effective. Then, in the Effective column, list the qualities, approaches and/or modalities that made each trainer or teacher effective. Now take time to think about the three worst trainers or teachers you ever had to learn from.

List their names or initials in the Worst Trainer column. Then, in the Ineffective column, list the qualities, approaches, and/or modalities that made each one ineffective in delivering learning. Take a look at your completed chart. Are there learning approaches, qualities, techniques and/or tools that you'd like to see duplicated for the training for your team? Are there some that you want to ensure are not duplicated for your team?

After you have taken time to think about what you'd like to keep and implement – and what you'd like to throw away - list the action you want to take for each quality or approach listed in the Action column. For items you want to avoid, you can write something like "throw away" or "lose it." For items, you want to implement on your team, write the specific action you'd like to take. Remember, you can always revisit this chart and update it as your team and your company evolves. Be sure to keep the worksheet – and the names or initials listed on it – private.

The E.T.: The Effective Trainer				
Best Trainer	Worst Trainer	Effective	Ineffective	Action

158

HR Fundamentals for Non-HR Managers: Can We Be Friends? (& CYA!)

BUILDING A WINNING TEAM

A GREAT TEAM NEEDS A GREAT COACH

Formal training is only one element of a learning strategy.

Key Terms and Definitions

Manager as Coach – Having regular, brief one-on-one discussions to help employees improve.

Career Pathing – Helping employees discover and achieve their career goals.

The Issue

In the previous chapter we talked about the importance of training, however, training isn't enough. Employees need a certain amount of ongoing coaching if they are to stay motivated and develop the necessary skills.

Coaching shouldn't just be about doing today's job. You should also help employees think about their career path and enable them to grow in their existing role, move laterally to a new role, or move up to a bigger role.

A Short Story

Simeon was a manager at Eezie Engineering. He was always the life of the party. Most of his colleagues would describe him as a bright, forward-thinking, and formidable presence. He had helped grow the firm from start-up to IPO and always went "full steam ahead" without waiting for others to catch up. During staff meetings, Simeon would always speak first, and with authority. After he spoke, his team appeared reluctant to contribute to the conversation at all (*Tap mic* Is this thing on?). When a team member did speak up to pose a question, Simeon would abruptly interrupt and interject before hearing the complete question.

> **Coach your team to greatness.**
> **Must haves: head and heart**

Adam, Simeon's VP, could see that Simeon's effectiveness as a manager was inhibited by his behaviors. He heard from Simeon's team that they dread the meetings and feel unappreciated. Of course, Simeon, on the whole, was a successful manager so he didn't want to come down too hard on him. Adam did bring this to Simeon's attention, but Simeon wouldn't hear it (and not because he had his earbuds in); he just didn't believe it was a serious problem.

As the VP, Adam wondered what he should do. He made a list of the options:

- He could send Simeon on a training program.

- He could order Simeon to stop being a jerk in meetings.

- He could give Simeon time to learn on his own; after all, he was still developing as a manager.

- He could ignore it for now and focus on other priorities.

Adam wondered if he was missing any options.

It Starts with your Heart

Do you genuinely care about your team? Coaching them from a place of authenticity is critical, as authors Daniel Harkavay and Steve Halliday note in their book, *Becoming a Coaching Leader,*

Heart is the difference maker in great leaders. You cannot be a great coach without heart. If you don't genuinely care about people - if you are coldly tactical and distantly technical and efficiently process oriented and leave your heart out of it,- then your people will follow you only part of the way. They need to believe that by following you, they will go places they would not even see without you at the helm. [43]

So sure, one reason you coach is to improve productivity, but at heart, it's about heart. This is all about humans, so connect to your team members on a human-to-human level when you begin to coach.

If you connect well then you'll be able to get the most out of your workforce. Many managers do not. Clifton and Harter point out:

> It's no surprise that organizations aren't getting the most out of their workforces. Less than 30% of managers strongly agree that someone at work encourages their development. According to the people receiving manager development training, the programs in place don't work. [44]

Why It Can Be Hard to Start with your Heart

We expect that you agree that it's sensible to "start with your heart." We all want to be open, transparent, honest, and humble. Unfortunately, that can be hard to do. Managers often feel they have to take on a certain persona as a leader and that ends up making them less than fully authentic. Managers might worry that they won't be able to say the right things or give the right impressions. Some managers suffer from "imposter syndrome" where they feel they are not fully qualified for the

role and are afraid that if they are open and authentic then they'll be called out.

There are many reasons why coaching from the heart can be hard. All we care about right now is why it might be hard for you personally and what you can do about it. So ask yourself these questions:

- How comfortable are you coaching your employees?

- What might be hindering you from being open?

- How can you make at least one little step towards overcoming the barriers that prevent you from coaching from the heart?

How to Coach

True or false, no one has time to do coaching? (Especially you.) If you said "true," we'll give you a half-mark if you meant, "I don't have time to sit down with employees for hour-long sessions helping them figure out their life." You only get half a point because that's not how effective coaching by managers works. Coaching by managers involves short sessions.

> ## Don't use the excuse that you don't have time to coach. It's your job, not theirs.

Michael Bungay Stanier, the author of *The Coaching Habit: Say Less, Ask More, & Change the Way You Lead Forever*, suggests that coaching sessions should only take five minutes. Now answer this question, "Can you spend five minutes once a week coaching each employee?" Unless you have a huge team, then the answer is certainly, "Yes."

Stanier goes on to say that you don't even have to know the answers to be a good coach. Just ask your employees questions about what's on their mind, what the challenges are, what the options are, and so on. More often than not they can figure things out on their own.

In fact, Stanier goes even further in suggesting you refrain from offering advice (he warns about "The Advice Monster"). This makes your life even easier as you don't need to solve everything; you only need to support the employee in overcoming their own obstacles.

Authors and coaches, Marshall Goldsmith and Laurence Lyons, agree. In their book, *Coaching for Leadership: The Practice of Leadership Coaching from the World's Greatest Coaches*, as they state,

> The directional or strategic power of any coaching dialogue lives primarily in its ability to question. Questions may be asked to surface submerged issues or may be asked to help the executive to reconsider some position or proposed course of action...[45]

Meanwhile, Coach U Inc. tells us more about the exchange of value in their foundational book, *The Coach U Personal and Corporate Coach Training Handbook*, which states,

> ## Coaching is more about asking good questions than it is about giving advice.

162

HR Fundamentals for Non-HR Managers: Can We Be Friends? (& CYA!)

At the heart of coaching is the exchange of value between you and the coachee, facilitated through the listening process. Solid listening skills are a part of the toolbox of an effective coach. Listening to another person for the purpose of his or her growth involves knowing how and when to listen and respond, what to listen for, what the coachee's words mean, and when it's appropriate to move the conversation in another direction. Listening is more of an art than a science; you cannot learn to listen perfectly, but through intentional practices you can greatly improve your skill. [46]

Coach yourself by reflecting on your existing coaching skills.

Coaching at a Distance

If your employees are in a different location, working from home or on the road, then coaching simply requires some different methods than in a face-to-face setting. The principles are the same; it's just that you can't pop into the cab of a truck barreling down the interstate to ask a driver, "What's on your mind?"

The solution to this is two-fold. First, there is the obvious: phone calls, text messaging, video conferencing, and occasional visits. The second part is harder and really depends on your commitment to improving performance. The second part is making time to coach people who are out of your sightline. It's relatively easy to find opportunities to coach someone you walk by five times a day. Those kinds of opportunities don't spontaneously occur for people who are not in your location. You'll have to build a schedule of check-in communications, and use those as opportunities to coach. That discipline is what will make you a spectacularly successful manager.

Take a Moment to Reflect on your Coaching Skills

As always, just a little self-reflection can go a long way to improving your management skills. Ask yourself the following:

- How can you coach your team to achieve team and company goals?

- What is your current coaching style (if you have one)?

- Is your present coaching style effective? If you believe so, what evidence reveals this?

- If not, what can you change about your approach to make it more effective?

Being Fair in Coaching

Who do you spend the most time coaching? Is it the employees you don't like? Is it employees you don't feel really comfortable around? Unless you are some kind of saint, this won't be the case. (If you are a saint, feel free to skip to the next section.)

Be careful that you use your coaching time fairly. We say 'fairly' instead of 'equally' because there are some people who benefit much more from coaching than others, and you want the highest return on investment in your coaching time. We can't give you a formula for fairness; only you can look at your own behavior to see if some employees are being overlooked.

Career Pathing (looking ahead)

There should be a natural step from coaching employees about how to do their existing job and coaching them for their next job. Yes, they love working for you now, but they may not want to work for you forever. Most employees have ambitions of moving up the ladder at least a rung or two. As a manager, you owe it to them to help with that process.

Hey, it may feel as if you are shooting yourself in the foot to help one of your good employees move to a new role, but not to worry. If you show an employee you care about their career, they are more motivated and more productive. Besides, most will not work for you

forever whether or not you do career coaching, so you might as well try to help them move up or laterally within your organization rather than looking for opportunities elsewhere. A great manager is one who coaches their team members to one day replace them! (Or who helps them get where they want to go in their career.)

The Nature of Career Paths

Think about careers. How often do they progress in a series of straightforward, predictable steps? How often do new opportunities arise in totally

unexpected ways? Since so much in life is unpredictable, you will not be able to give a clear career map for most employees. You are likely to find that you will have three main categories of employees:

1. Employees in roles where the next step in their career is pretty clear

2. Employees where the next step is clear but getting there appears unlikely

3. Employees where you have no clue what their next step up could be

164

HR Fundamentals for Non-HR Managers: Can We Be Friends? (& CYA!)

The first category, the clear ones, includes employees that have a pretty traditional career path where there is an existing job ladder. Job ladders are quite common. There might be a path of Junior Clerk to Clerk to Senior Clerk. In this case, it's pretty easy for you to explain to an employee what they need to do to progress.

The second category, where making the next step up is unlikely, will be harder for you to deal with. It might be the case that there is a clear path such as store clerk to store assistant manager to store manager. However, there may be twenty store clerks and only one assistant manager, so few will make it up to that next rung. Sure, you can talk to your twenty store clerks about this career path, but most will recognize that it's not particularly realistic.

> Ensure you have provided robust career pathing. The rest is up to your team. #TeamFlourish

The third category, the unclear ones, are jobs where there is no obvious next step. Maybe you have a forklift driver and you can't think of a bigger job this person would ever be qualified for—unless it's driving a bigger forklift (and you don't have any bigger forklifts).

How To Coach Employees on Career Paths

Where your employees are on a job ladder, it's not too hard to manage coaching conversations. You do need to have a discussion with them about their career interests (which may not be on the ladder); you do need to explain what it takes to move up to the next step, and you do need to support them in acquiring the skills. Okay, you know all that, we'll leave you to it. Go and schedule some career discussions if you've not done so.

For the jobs with no obvious career ladder, you need to take a slightly different tactic. Again, start with the conversation. What are your ambitions? What do you like doing? What are your interests? Be honest with them that either there are no obvious next steps or the competition for that next step is fierce, but tell them you'll work with them to figure it out. Think about extra projects they could take on; introduce them to managers in other departments where they might be a lateral move; encourage them to explore their interests and learn more about other jobs in the company.

The reality of careers is that many moves are lateral, opportunistic and some are wildly unexpected. You can't hand an employee a career path on a silver platter, but you can be encouraging, inventive, and supportive.

All you have to do is have conversations with your employees about their career interests, and then do your best to help them explore ways to get ahead. It's their career; they'll figure it out, but as their manager, you should be a source of ideas and support.

Thinking Outside the Box

One of the barriers to having meaningful career discussions is that we think inside the box of "What is the next job up in this department?" That problem is too large for that little box. We're gonna need a bigger box! The bigger box includes project work, volunteer work at a charitable organization, and temporary lateral moves. All those things can be options for moving someone towards their career goals.

Another barrier to meaningful discussions is that employees don't have a good idea of what they want or what options exist. Those same tactics of getting people involved in things that are new to them (projects, charitable work, etc.) will help people see new possibilities for their life and career.

Clifton and Harter have an interesting way of describing this process of helping people see new possibilities in *It's The Manager*,

Employees develop through the discoveries they make as they perform and as they are coached. Managers should ask themselves: How can I encourage individuals to make more discoveries about themselves? Remember, different employees see growth and development differently. One may see winning internal awards as career growth, while another may think getting an advanced degree is more valuable. One employee may view travel and bigger client presentations as a step up, while another may want to be a mentor. [47]

If you approach career discussions as a process of discovery, it's a lot more fun than if you think you need to specify exactly how and when an employee will get their next promotion.

Being Fair in Career Discussions

There is a problem with discussing careers with your employees. It is a place where subtle (or sometimes not so subtle!) biases can run rampant. Do you tell the good looking young employee with the nice suit that they could well be the next CEO? Do you tell the hard-working person from a poor family that they might enjoy a lateral move, but only after they've proven themselves?

So let's take an unpleasant moment of self-reflection. Think about each of your employees and what potential career path you see each taking. Now think about how much that assessment of potential is based on superficial aspects of their style, background, or personality? If you are like most humans, superficial matters often play a big role in your view of someone's potential. But in the end, you won't be like most managers; you'll be one of the really good ones.

The main trick here is not to presume too much in your discussion about careers. Use a coaching mindset and ask a lot of questions. Answer their questions. Encourage them to strive to achieve what they want. Your job is to help each individual be their best. You don't need to predict how high (or in which direction) they will go.

Take a Moment To Reflect on your Ability to Coach Career Pathing

Are you doing a great job of helping employees navigate their careers? Maybe not, many managers struggle with this. Here are some questions to help you improve your approach:

Partner with HR (and CYA)

Help HR by being scrupulously unbiased in your career pathing discussions and don't make assumptions about people based on stereotypes or superficial factors.

- List each of your employees. When was the last time you had a brief chat about their career goals?

- How effectively do you feel you help your team navigate their career paths to meet their career goals?

- Can you think of creative ways to help people move towards their career goals?

- What creative ways can you think of to help people broaden their horizons and discover new career goals?

Back to the Story

Adam bumped into his HR business partner in the hallway and asked her about finding a training program for Simeon on how to run a meeting. The HR professional didn't rush off to find a program; instead, she asked Adam to describe the issue in more detail. The HR pro then said, "Have you considered coaching Simeon?"

Well, that was a fresh idea. HR went on to suggest a useful exercise for Simeon would be to monitor how much of the meeting he spent speaking versus listening, as well as how often people were interrupted and who did the interrupting.

Adam quietly sat in on one of Simeon's meetings and made notes of who was speaking and who was interrupting.

Afterward, he spent a few minutes with Simeon showing him how it could be useful to monitor the meeting process. He didn't spend a lot of time telling Simeon that he needed to do things differently, but the look on Simeon's face when he realized he did 80% of the talking and 100% of the interrupting showed that he got the point that there was room for improvement.

Summing Up

Coaching is one of the most important things you do as a manager. Keep in mind that:

- You don't need to do long sit-down coaching meetings; five minutes here and there is much more practical.

- Coaching is generally more about asking questions than giving advice.

- Coaching covers many things: encouragement, problem-solving, clarity on priorities, etc. Your focus depends on the situation.

- Coaching about today's work should transition to talking about the employee's career. It's something you should touch on once a year.

- Be careful to avoid the natural human tendency to show favoritism in coaching and career discussions.

That's enough content; now let's take a break and do a brief activity that will help you with career pathing.

> Help employees experience new things that will open their eyes to potential career paths.

The Compass: A Career Pathing Activity

For this activity, you will work with your team members individually. Set aside 20 minutes during a one-on-one to first introduce the activity and answer any questions about it. Remind each individual that there are no "right or wrong answers." Then, provide each team member with a copy of the **Career Pathing Action Plan** below (hard or soft copy). Invite the team member to set aside time to honestly and reflectively complete the worksheet. Team members should be allotted one week to work on the activity privately and individually.

After team members have had an opportunity to complete the Career Pathing Action Plan, meet with them individually to review their completed worksheets. As your team member shares their results, write their responses down in the My Goals column. Then, encourage them to share their thoughts on how the goals listed in the **My Goals** column can be achieved. Write each idea for how goals can be achieved in the **Career Path Action Plan** column. Take time to discuss each response.

When you are done, schedule time to meet again to review their goals as they grow along their career paths.

Career Pathing Worksheet			
	Description	My Goals	Career Path Steps
Current Role	What role do you currently hold?		
Pinnacle Role	The role you see yourself in at the pinnacle of your career. Your "dream job."		
Is it ideal?	Why is your pinnacle role ideal for you?		
Qualifications needed?	What qualifications are needed for the role?		

ENERGIZING EMPLOYEES

RECOGNITION, APPRECIATION, AND INSPIRATION

Partner with HR (and CYA)

HR wants you to show employees that you appreciate their hard work. This will go a long way to preventing undue problems in retention, motivation and attitudes.

Key Terms and Definitions

Recognition – praise or tangible awards for an accomplishment

Appreciation – heartfelt show that an employee's ongoing efforts are valued

Inspiration – energize employees to reach new levels of excellence

The Issue

Employees who love working for you are wonderful to have around. You have three main tools to make working for you a delight: recognition, appreciation and inspiration. These three approaches are all related but there are some distinctions worth paying attention to.

Recognition is usually tied to specific accomplishments such as being employee of the month, having reached a 10-year anniversary, or making a special effort to help a client. This is good for reinforcing desired behaviors.

Appreciation, which has to be heartfelt to be effective, involves frequently letting the employee know that you value their hard work, their contributions and that you're aware of the difficulties they overcome each day. This is good for building commitment.

Inspiration is about setting an example and a vision that encourages employees to reach a new standard of excellence. This is good for elevating performance over the long run.

What these all have in common is that they help employees love working for you and encourage them to perform well as a result. As a manager you will be more successful if you learn the simple skills of recognition and appreciation. You will be very successful if you master the art of inspiration.

A Short Story

Ms. Malhotra, CEO of M-Smart Enterprises stepped onto a plane in Atlanta on her way to a Board meeting in Los Angeles. Smartly dressed and with a new carry-on bag in tow, she made her way through the business class seats. She nodded to Mr. Perez, CFO for a Boston-based financial firm. She gave her best wishes to Ms. LaFleur who runs the US operations of a European manufacturer. She smiled warmly at Mr. Anderson, a corporate lawyer she's done business with. All the while she

A leader's day to day behavior can be a powerful source of inspiration.

kept walking. She passed right through business class and made her way to a seat in economy class.

Part way through the flight, Mr. Anderson came back to see her. "Oh my heavens, it's cramped back here. It's such a shame business class was sold out and you were relegated to sitting with the riff-raff. I'm going to send you the name of my travel agent. He's

fantastic. He always finds a business class seat for me even at the busiest times."

Ms. Malhotra thanked him for his kindness and paused. Should she say anything or not? She didn't want to make him look bad in any way, but she did have something important she wanted to explain.

"Mr. Anderson, I want to share a little secret with you", she said. He looked momentarily aghast. "No, it's not what you're thinking, I still have my job and the company is doing very well." Anderson was relieved. "You see, my secret is that I always fly economy. I don't make a big deal about it, but people see me and talk about it and my employees know. I want to live in a culture where we are all on one team. This is just one of the ways I try to show it. When all my employees can fly business class, then I will too. Until then you'll find me here because in the end, I'm just a team member along with everyone else."

Anderson was impressed, but as he walked away he decided he must never pass on the name of his travel agent to Ms. Malhotra. If the travel agent learned that the CEO of M-Smart Enterprises flew economy, then he might not work so hard to ensure Anderson got a business class seat. He dodged a bullet there! He relaxed back into his seat and ordered another champagne.

Ms. Malhotra didn't have champagne, but we bet she did have inspired employees.

Recognition
What Do We Mean by Rewards and Recognition? (It's a trick, sorry)

We are going to have to apologize for HR here. HR will talk to you about "Total Rewards"; they'll also talk to you about "Rewards and Recognition." You're probably thinking it's nothing new as you have already learned about rewards. Sorry, but not so fast. When we say rewards, as in "total rewards," we usually mean something kinda different from when we just say rewards, as in "rewards and recognition." It's confusing, and to make matters worse not everyone uses the terms in the same way. It's just one of those things.

Let's explain as best we can. First, your company may have a VP of Total Rewards (that's the same thing as a VP of Compensation and Benefits, but it sounds cooler). They will devote almost all of their effort to base pay, different kinds of incentive pay, and benefits. These are the big ticket items that are the main reasons employees show up on Monday mornings.

Compliance Do's and Don'ts

- Absolutely do not show bias or favoritism in how you give recognition.

Secondly, the *concept* of Total Rewards includes everything that employees value including things like good learning opportunities and a great workplace. Normally the VP of Total Rewards doesn't handle those other things, they just do compensation and benefits.

Finally, rewards and recognition programs usually refer to things where employees who accomplish something get:

- small awards (such as a gift card or merchandise),
- an employee of the month plaque (or similar public acknowledgement),
- a token for years of service, or
- simply praise for a job well done.

Recognition may be managed by HR, but it might also be managed by Operations or some other department; it varies from place to place. Sorry for that long explanation but it's best to get the confusion out of the way. (Whew!)

> Just as "no bad deed shall go unnoticed," there should be accolades for every accomplishment. Bring on the rewards! And, have a little fun while you are at it!

Why Give Recognition?

Look, you're paying someone right? Why do you need to tell them they're doing a good job? The answer, as is so often the case in management, is that employees are human. Maybe a monthly paycheck should be enough to keep them motivated, but the fact is you get a lot better performance if you give people the occasional pat on the back--and all the better if that pat is accompanied by something tangible, like movie tickets.

Even more important than *general* motivation is the *specific* behavior that you give them a pat on the back for. If there is a behavior you want to see more of, then you have to encourage it. You encourage it by showing some recognition when you see desirable behaviors.

Who Is Responsible for Rewards and Recognition? (Mainly you.)

Your company might have a formal rewards and recognition program. Often there is a website you can use to give a spot award to a deserving employee. Sometimes these are points systems where employees are given recognition points that they can cash in for a gift of their choice.

Okay, that's what someone else was responsible for setting up. What are *you* responsible for doing? You are responsible for using recognition in an effective manner. This is the case whether or not there is a formal rewards and recognition program. If you don't have a website that issues awards, you can always give a word of praise, a handwritten note, or buy a pizza for a hard-working team.

The success of recognition in driving the right behaviors is almost entirely up to you. It's a powerful tool, but only you can make it an effective tool for your team. Let's talk more about how to do that.

What Makes Recognition Work?

Let's do a mini-exercise here to make a point. How do you feel when:

- You've moved mountains to keep a client after someone mightily screwed up. The next week you see an email from your boss telling you that you earned 100 reward points.

- Your boss tells you, "Yeah, you've done a decent job on a bunch of stuff over the past few months so good work."

- At your 20-year anniversary you find a cheap plaque on your desk titled "20 Years."

> A handwritten note can work wonders.

In all these cases there is recognition, but it doesn't have much impact. Imagine instead if:

- Your boss writes a handwritten note and couriers it to your home with some rewards points as "a small token of appreciation" on the same day that you fixed a problem.

- Your boss stops by to say thank you for how you specially tuned yesterday's presentation so that the people from finance would buy in.

- Your boss gathers everyone together and makes a short speech outlining some key moments in your 20 year career before handing you the plaque to commemorate the day.

If you want your recognition to drive motivation and the right behaviors, then the recognition needs to be:

- Specific - be precise about which behavior is being recognized

- Timely - give recognition when the behavior happens (not months later!)

- Sincere - put some heart into how you give recognition so employees know you care

Frankly, all you need to do is put yourselves in the shoes of the person you want to acknowledge. Make a small effort to get each act of recognition right, and you'll find you get much better performance.

How Recognition Programs Can Go Wrong

If you don't put any personal care into recognition awards, they can be ineffective. Worse still, they can actually do harm. Here are some things to worry about:

- Do employees believe that recognition is based on favoritism?

- Do employees who don't get recognized feel demotivated?

- Do employees who get recognized feel like they are being treated like children being rewarded with a cookie for good behavior instead of a professional who does excellent work as a matter of course?

What's the easy way to avoid these problems? When you find out, please let us know! The best advice we can give is to be sensitive to these concerns. You know your team so use your instincts to avoid missteps. Note how people are reacting and make sure people understand your intention. When they understand your intention, they are more likely to interpret recognition in a positive way.

> Do you appreciate your employees' efforts? Then let them know.

> "There is a huge difference between, recognition and gratitude. The difference for me is the personal and emotional connection. Recognition is often the award, the thing. And those are important. Gratitude gets to the heart and soul of a person. Recognition is often an event, gratitude is a relationship." [48]

> Who do you personally know who inspires you?

Appreciation
(a deeper level)

There is a different way of approaching recognition. It's the idea that what we want is to show appreciation for the person and their work. There is just a subtle difference here. Recognition can be seen as a kind of quid pro quo; for example, if I come in for four weeks with no absences, then I earn a box of donuts. Appreciation emphasizes the personal side.

Chester Elton, co-author with Adrian Gostick of the best selling *Leading with Gratitude: Eight Leadership Practices for Extraordinary Business Results* thinks that the heart of the matter (pun intended) lies in gratitude as he stated in conversation,

What you are trying to communicate is that you, as their manager, genuinely appreciate the effort your team makes to arrive on time every day: that you are grateful for the work they put into that presentation, and that you appreciate the fact that they've been loyal to the company for 20 years.

Appreciation and recognition programs can go hand in hand. Just keep this idea of appreciation top of mind; we think you'll find that it makes you a better manager.

Inspiration
(the highest goal)

Would you like to develop into the kind of manager who inspires people? That's an ambitious goal, but a goal worth striving for. You might think it takes some sort of inborn charisma to be able to inspire others but that's not the case. The ability to inspire is a skill you can develop. Let's think about how you might embark on the path to being inspiring.

As is so often the case, a good place to start is with yourself. What inspires you? Who inspires you? Think about people you actually know, not a historical figure. (We want you to be inspiring, but we don't expect you to be Martin Luther King Jr.)

Next ask your employees. Who in their life do they find inspirational? When have they been inspired? You'll learn a lot about inspiration that way. You'll also learn a lot about your employees.

One thing you'll notice is that an individual doesn't need to be super-duper extraordinary to inspire people. Employees may be inspired by a sales manager they had who had forgotten more about selling than they would ever know. They may be inspired by the busy manager who somehow always made time for every employee. They may be inspired by the manager who never gives up, even when the going gets tough.

So could you be inspiring one day? For sure. Be a good role model, be skilled and diligent about what you do, be persistent and consistent. Keep working on those attributes and they can elevate you from the average manager to the inspiring one.

Another side of inspiration is the big vision. Let's go back to the vision statement of the Princess Margaret Cancer Centre we mentioned in the very first chapter. Their vision is to "Conquer Cancer in Our Lifetime". This is what Jim Collins, author of Good to Great, calls a BHAG: a Big Hairy Audacious Goal.

In your own department you may not be able to come up with a BHAG, but we bet you can come up with a GYHOOTS. This acronym, GYHOOTS, is one we just made up. It means "Get your head out of the swamp." Employees can get so bogged down in the swamp of daily work that they can't see further than the next email. You can help inspire them by reminding them of why they are doing what they're doing, why it matters to the customers, and why you are proud of what the team is striving to achieve. Remind your employees to look up and see the good things they are achieving. Let them know they too should be proud.

Inspiration is a matter of showing employees that they can follow in the footsteps of someone they admire, and that they can be a part of a team doing awesome work. If you're lucky, the inspiration can be that the organization is pursuing some world changing goal, but the point is, you don't need that amazing goal; you can inspire just by being an excellent manager.

Help employees get their heads out of the swamp of day to day work so they can enjoy the greater vision. #GYHOOTS

> Recognition needs to be sincere to be effective. Find at least one small thing you appreciate about each team member.

Summing Up

Most people are familiar with recognition programs. We can build on recognition by venturing into appreciation and ultimately inspiration. Here are some key points:

- Recognition needs to be sincere to be effective.

- Recognition should be specific and timely.

- While recognition follows after the employee accomplishes some specific objective, appreciation shows up in more general day-to-day communication. It's about showing that you notice the ongoing contributions employees make and that you are grateful.

- Inspiration is a matter of consistently behaving in a way that employees want to emulate.

That's not complicated is it? Take it to heart. Now let's try an exercise:

Back to the Story

We've all seen too many movies where inspiration comes in the form of stirring speech. That's misleading. For leaders like Ms. Malhotra inspiration flowed from how she simply lived the values of the organization. She was a leader and a person whom her employees would like to emulate.

Showing that you appreciate employees, doing great work yourself, and living the values are all ways to get the best from your team. Don't worry if you're not the type to stand on a chair and enrapture the crowd with a rousing speech. You can inspire just by being the best version of yourself.

Appreciating the Individual:
Grow the Spirit

This activity prepares you to be better at recognition by starting with appreciation. As humans, we are more aware of what people do that frustrates us, rather than of the good things they do. Let's take a moment to stoke the fires of appreciation by thinking about those good things.

List the names of each member of your team in the **Team Member** column below. Then, write in a **Positive Personality Trait** they have (e.g. reliable) and **Something They're Good At** (e.g. good with numbers).

Now go back and read what you've written. Can you feel a sense of appreciation for what each individual brings to the team? If so, you'll be better prepared to show appreciation and more inclined to give recognition.

(Are there some employees you struggle to appreciate? Maybe take the time to ask other people about what they like about them.)

Team Member	Positive Trait	Something They're Good At

SECTION 7

Leading Your Team Doesn't Have
To Be Like Herding Cats!

CREATE A WINNING TEAM

EXCEL AT TEAM BUILDING

> Many teams are not effective; it's up to the manager to figure out why.

Key Terms and Definitions

Effective Team Work – Getting more productivity from a team than you would if they each worked alone.

Storming – A normal phase of discord shortly after a team is initially formed.

The Issue

A great deal of work is done in teams. As we know from (bitter?) experience, not all teams are effective. Managers can make a difference if they pay attention to team building and team dynamics, so that they get their teams on the right track.

A Short Story

Gus managed a regional office and needed a website so that customers could sign up for events he was putting on. He asked Hans from IT, Stephanie from Marketing, and Sao from Customer Success to form a team to whip up a website. The meeting went a bit like this:

Stephanie began the meeting. "I've got some ideas about designing the content so that it aligns with the brand. What are your thoughts on IT, Hans?"

Hans said, "I can code up a flexible system in JavaScript with some help from that consultant we used last time to ensure it works with different mobile devices."

Stefani, "Geez, Hans you want to turn everything into some big IT adventure. My nephew used something called FreeWebWonder for a school project and got it done in an afternoon. Let's use that."

Hans said, "I'm not sure that will give us the flexibility we need, but I'll do whatever the team decides. What do you think, Sao?"

Sao said, "Wait a minute, I've got to take this call."

Stephanie said, "I'll get a press release out telling customers that this will be ready in two weeks."

Hans replied, "We might want to run some tests before we go live with customers, but if you think Gus needs it that fast, I suppose we can take the risk."

"Good. That's decided," said Stefani, "What's your view Sao?"

"Umm, just a sec….Can you repeat that? I just needed to send out an email, and I missed part of the discussion," said Sao.

Stephanie explained, "Hans was just saying he'll have the site fully ready in two weeks using FreeWebWonder. What's your take on this from the customer's perspective?"

Sao looked up from her phone. "Well, I'm sure it's fine. Look we're running out of time here, and I've got a meeting to prepare for, so let's take this up another day."

Partner with HR (and CYA)

Touch base with HR on any team building tools or frameworks you want to use. There may be standard ones the company has already adopted or paid for.

Gus's dysfunctional team was not off to a good start, and there was little reason to think it would get better on its own. He was going to have to do something to improve teamwork on this project.

Is Team Building Fun and Games?

When asked to describe "team building," you may think about obstacle courses, scavenger hunts, and "trust" exercises like falling backwards with eyes closed, hoping (praying!) to get "caught." Or, perhaps you envision "hanging" together for things like movie night, beer pong, fun runs, etc.. These activities might help people get to know each other outside of their cubicles, but how does this translate into building effective relationships that enhance productivity?

Besides, let's face it. The majority of the team may not even want to participate in a typical team building activity. In fact, you can rest assured that many staff members may leave that event thinking, "I'll never get that day in my life back again." As stated by Theresa Agovino in her article, *Building Team Bonds,*

Nearly a third of employees said that team building was an office event they secretly dislike, tied with baby showers, according to a survey conducted by Wakefield Research for Citrix Systems, Inc. They were second only to costume parties on the list of events that workers would rather skip. [49]

There are times when these kinds of activities can work to help people get to know one another, however, they are generally not the best approach to team building.

Is Team Building a Social Event?

Some approaches to team building *do* emphasize fun social events. This doesn't mean pulling pranks like placing a co-worker's paper clips in Jell-O or plastic wrapping their chair. But aspects of intentionally incorporating fun can be helpful. Your initial approach may involve Muffin Mondays and Casual Fridays, which everyone loves! However, when it comes to fun, people predictably like to hang out with the people who are most like them, because it's more comfortable. They rarely interact with the other team members at work. As a result, these social events only strengthen bonds between people who are already friends; they don't do a great job of building new friendships.

If you are hoping that social events will help people on the team who are not already friends become friends, then you'll have to take some steps to force them to mix. The easiest way to do this is to have a meal (we're thinking pizza in the lunchroom, not dinner at a Michelin restaurant) with assigned seating to get the kind of mixing you want. Make sure team members know that the purpose of the social is to build new connections, so that they understand why they are assigned a seat.

Compliance Do's and Don'ts

- Do check with safety professionals if you are doing any physical activity where an employee could get hurt.
- Don't do anything that will embarrass an employee.

182

HR Fundamentals for Non-HR Managers: Can We Be Friends? (& CYA!)

Develop Teamwork Skills

Okay, enough of the fun stuff. What about some serious skill building? The most common approach to improving teamwork skills is to help people appreciate that others have different strengths, styles, viewpoints, preferences, and shortcomings. Intellectually, we all know this is true, however when people are put through an exercise assessing and discussing individual differences, then it really strikes home.

When an employee identifies their own personality traits and is reminded just how different other people's personalities can be, it can then give them the "aha" moment of why they don't always get along. People begin to see the way someone else behaves as a trait rather than a flaw. A "big picture" person will recognize that their teammate who keeps asking for details is not doing so to be annoying. It's just how they make sense of things. They'll also come to realize that having at least one detail-oriented person on the team is extremely valuable.

> **Personality assessment exercises can create "aha" moments.**

There are many different assessment methods that give people insight into personality traits. Ask HR if they have a tool or framework that they've successfully used in the company. Popular frameworks like Myers-Briggs are not particularly scientific, but the point usually isn't so much about accuracy as it is to get people thinking about themselves and others, and to have some common language to describe the differences. A high performing team needs to have individual members recognize that they each have their unique core strengths that can contribute to a common goal.

Is an Offsite Team Building Meeting a Good Idea?

Sometimes it takes changing the environment to isolate opportunities for each employee so that they have a better understanding of themselves and others. That's why offsite team building can be valuable. It may also be a good opportunity to bring in remote workers so that they can socialize face to face with everyone else.

Note that if you do have a significant number of remote workers and you cannot bring them in, you have two main options:

- Run a video call 'offsite' just for the remote workers. Cover the same content but adapt it for the video call. You will want to break it up into several two-hour sessions rather than try to do it all in one day, since video calls are tiring.

- Do the whole meeting 'offsite' as a video experience for everyone. Employees who are normally onsite can do the calls from home or the office. The advantage of this approach is that everyone has the same experience.

What do you do in an offsite, virtual, or other type of meeting? Usually it's a relaxed day with a series of exercises and lectures around team building. Be clear what you most want to accomplish, and then work with HR or a consultant to map out the agenda for the day.

If an offsite session isn't practical, don't worry. You can make progress in helping team members understand one another's unique personalities in a one-hour session by video conferencing or in the office. Note that if you are doing this kind of meeting with remote workers, don't ask them to be on the video while everyone else is face-to-face. Do a video call with everyone so that they all have the same experience.

Focusing on Team Performance

As well as looking at the personality differences that affect team dynamics, it can be helpful to spend time talking directly about the team's goals. Sit the team down in front of a whiteboard and

> **Don't assume a team member knows what other team members are doing.**

map out each member's role and how they contribute to the project. You may assume everyone already knows this, but you'll be surprised how clueless people can be about what their team members actually do.

Another good tactic to get the team focused on performance is to have daily huddles where everyone has a chance to speak. There are three questions you'll want to ask in these huddles:

- Where are we? (don't spend too much time on this because frankly it gets boring)

- What do we need to do and who will do it, and by when? (this is the guts of the meeting)

- Is there anything in how we are operating as a team that is getting in the way of achieving our goals? (this is often overlooked)

You can see now that team building has various dimensions. There is the fun and social side, and then there is the serious side of understanding personality and focusing on the work itself. If all goes well, this will lead to a successful team. But what if it's not successful? Keep reading; we've got that covered.

Understanding Why Teams Fail

We've been focusing on the positive side of team building such as building social bonds and recognizing personality differences. How about we look at it from another angle: why teams fail. An extremely popular book on teams is Patrick Lencioni's *The Five Dysfunctions of a Team*. Lencioni says that the most significant causes of dysfunction in team dynamics are:

- absence of trust,
- fear of conflict,
- lack of commitment,
- avoidance of accountability, and
- inattention to results. [50]

The order is important. If there is an absence of trust, you'll get nowhere. Once you have trust, you can address fear of conflict and so on. This framework can be useful for you in figuring out what's wrong with a team that isn't performing. The framework also helps you avoid jumping in to fix a problem that catches your attention (such as avoidance of accountability) when the underlying issue is something else (fear of conflict).

If you use this model to help teams that are in trouble, you'll eventually get to the point where you can foresee problems in advance. As a manager, getting this good sense of why teams fail and why they succeed is an important skill. You'll want to learn a number of frameworks and practice using them to hone your intuition.

> **If there is an absence of trust, you'll get nowhere.**

Understanding How Teams Evolve

We guess it's obvious that teams evolve over time. Have you ever thought about the stages of change? If not, no worries! Bruce Tuckman has looked at the stages of team formation. His framework has five stages:

1. Forming
2. Storming
3. Norming
4. Performing
5. Adjourning (or Transforming) [51]

That's a nice set of words that don't mean much alone, so let's see how Tuckman developed these ideas:

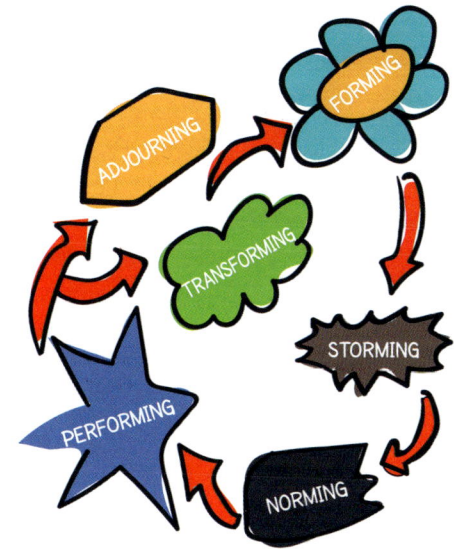

STAGES OF GROUP DEVELOPMENT

Forming

Forming is the first stage in team evolution. Often, the Forming Stage begins when a newly designed team meets for the first time. It is important to note that anytime you swap a team member, or one leaves the team, or another person is added, this is Forming. In this stage, team members are oriented to the project objectives and begin to think about what role they will play on the team.

There are a few steps you should take at the Forming Stage:

1. Get to know your team members; work to discover their skills, experience, and how they each best communicate.

2. As you identify the strengths of individuals, determine which role each person will fit best in.

3. Review your organization's culture, values, and longer-term objectives; share those with your newly formed (or re-formed) team.

4. Help to foster synergy and team alignment by ensuring your team sees how what they are working on ties to the organization's objectives; make sure everyone knows what they are working on matters!

The key to leading in the Forming Stage and building a winning team is to make sure each team member is clear on the goals and the role they will play.

Storming (don't worry — it's not "that" kind of storm!):

Storming is a natural stage in team development that you should be ready for. After Forming, team members often wonder, "Where do I fit on this team? What value am I expected to bring? How will we best work together? Do I matter? Which of us is supposed to step up and lead?"

Storming is the initial rough patch of weather as the team begins to work together. In a virtual team, sometimes team members also internally question, "How will we work effectively together when we work in different locations? Does my boss know what I am working on with this team? How will people know the value I contribute?"

On a team that has been re-shaped by the addition or removal of member(s), people from the earlier team may wonder or even ask you, "Am I still relevant on this team? Am I needed?"

As a manager, there are a few things you can proactively do to help your team get through the Storming stage:

1. As competition and conflict inevitably surface (put your boxing gloves away...you probably won't need them), assist the team in accepting individual differences, and working through conflicting ideas. Keep the team focused on the goals, and work through how to get there (and encourage egos to be checked at the door).

2. As the manager, be highly involved on the front end of a newly formed team's work. Help them overcome obstacles to healthy team dynamics by encouraging all to communicate early and often with one another.

3. Discuss processes that facilitate collective, creative problem-solving while affirming and appreciating contributions from all members.

4. Remind your newly formed team that conflict is normal in a team's development. Many times this helps decrease stress as teams navigate bumpy waters as folks find their way on the team.

The key to leading in the Storming Stage and building a winning team is to recognize, watch for, and provide assurances to team members that they matter, are valued, and wanted. This doesn't mean you have to hug everyone (please don't do hugs!) to express your appreciation for their contributions—simple words and gestures will go a long way! Remember that during this stage of team development, folks often are unsure if their work matters. Furthermore, conflict is normal as team members figure out where they fit. At times, some team members may feel like a square peg trying to fit into a round hole—ouch! Assuring the team that conflict is OK and even normal can be helpful. As the manager, it is your job to lead your team through 'Storming' to a new state of being (as a newly formed team).

Norming

Norming is the stage where things begin to come together. The team, often without even realizing it, begins to find pieces of a "new normal" as they create efficient processes and routines. The team settles into new ways of doing things as team members contribute in meaningful ways.

During the Norming Stage, you can support the process in these ways:

1 Encourage harmony and unity through discussion and collaboration on new processes and routines.

2 Focus on the team goals, and the essential contributions of the individual members. Remember to acknowledge how team members are establishing effective new norms.

3 Stabilize the processes; optimize what is working, eradicate what isn't. #SearchAndDestroy

The key to leading in the Norming stage and building a winning team is to help the team align with new processes that increase efficiency and effectiveness. During this phase, you will see team members contribute in meaningful ways. As the manager, affirm what works as your team finds a new "normal."

Performing

This is the stage where we see real results. This is when you feel your team is "cooking with grease." They are DOING what they were put together to do. As the Manager, in this stage, you need to:

1 Continue to build on the achievements of the team goals. Yes!

2 Be flexible; adapt the processes as needs evolve.

3 Keep the team focused on the objectives while continuing to optimize the process of getting there.

The key to leading in the Performing Stage and building a winning team is to celebrate milestones and key results as you achieve team objectives (yay team!!) Your affirmation of your team's performance may be the fuel that helps your team reach new and unexpected levels of achievement, while finding joy and harmony in the journey. Hold on... before you get out your tambourine, there's one more stage of team development.

Adjourning (or Transforming):

We know that all good things must come to an end. A team will either adjourn (end) because the purpose for which the team was formed has been met. Or the team may transform ("Form" again) when the group's members are changed. Effectively leading through this stage of your team may include using the following points:

1 Understand that your high-performing team <u>will</u> come to an end. This occurs either because the project finishes (Adjourning), or because people transition off or on the team (Transforming). Be direct with your team about this shift.

2 Team members may feel sad as they anticipate the "end of an era." Acknowledge this with your team. Encourage reflection on what has been great and what they may miss or want to re-create in the future on a different team.

3 Team members may feel stress as change to the team's status and work processes are imminent. Work to assure team members what you envision for their next responsibilities as the team they've been on will shift. #HandHolding-Time

The key to leading in the Adjourning or Transforming Stage includes recognizing that teams don't last forever.

Dr. Heidi Scott, HR.com's Chief Learning Officer, shares that,

The Adjourning Stage of a group's development is about closure. The season of this group working together toward its common purpose has come to an end. While we hope this is a time to celebrate because the group accomplished what it set out to do, and it built enjoyable relationships along the way, this is not always the case! Sometimes if a group has had an exceptionally challenging time working together (for many reasons), the fact that the group is breaking up may feel like the only cause for celebration.

Regardless, the time of Adjourning hopefully includes reflecting, assigning meaning from the process of the experience, and learning. [52]

188

HR Fundamentals for Non-HR Managers: Can We Be Friends? (& CYA!)

Similarly, the Transforming stage is,

> a unique stage of a group's development. It signals a change in its membership; individuals may leave while others enter the group. Either one of these elements changes the group's dynamics, creating a natural flow back to the first stage of Forming. The Transforming Stage may also come about from a change in the group's formal purpose. Or while a group maintains all of its members and it transitions to a new, focused project or endeavor, the shift in its needs for knowledge, skills, and expertise cause the group to transform. When a group works through the Transforming Stage, typically there are transition rituals involved; these may include a celebratory social event, awards related to the completed project or to exiting members, a formal debrief and learning meeting, or even individual nicknames being given. [52]

Your job as their manager is to help them say "Good bye" to the team as they've known it, to reflect, and to hopefully recognize personal lessons learned from the experience. Your team may be "transforming" to a new project or "transforming" as a team by adding some new members. (Grow team, grow!) Help your team capitalize on what they've learned about the team as they realize the team is transforming, and that they will most likely find themselves back at the Forming Stage.

Back to the Story

Our manager, Gus, thought he had an easy project. He put three people with different expertise on a straightforward task

> Often teams just gel without any special effort by the manager. That's great when it happens, but don't count on it.

and hoped the team would run with it. They were running with it, but they were running it into the ground not to a touchdown. It was a living example of a dysfunctional team.

Stephanie lacked trust in Hans; she didn't trust his technical ability and didn't trust he wouldn't turn it into a "tech adventure" rather than focus on the business needs. Hans was too afraid of conflict to defend his position. He would just go along with the team even if, as an expert, he was pretty sure it would lead to problems. Sao, due to her other work, had a major lack of commitment.

Sometimes you can just toss a team together, and it will work out. Sometimes it doesn't. Gus was learning that as a manager he needed to know how to set the team up for success, and how to intervene when things went wrong. Every team is different, so Gus will have to bring his wisdom and experience to keep each one on track.

Summing Up

Managers who build successful teams are managers who have just made their lives a whole lot easier. Some of the key ideas in this chapter are:

- Many people dislike the "fun and games" events that are often called "team building activities." Use them with caution.

- Social activities to build team bonds are generally good, but they tend to reinforce existing friendships rather than create new ones (so work to ensure new and deeper relationships are built among team members).

- Personality assessments that help team members understand their differences can be helpful in reducing conflict and misunderstandings.

- Keep an eye on the possible dysfunctions of your team (such as a lack of trust) which can undermine your team building efforts.

- Recognize that teams evolve through predictable stages over time. Be there to help them through this evolution.

Harvard Professor J. Richard Hackman has written a great deal about teams. When asked what drove this fascination, he said it was that he always found being on teams frustrating —and he wanted to know why. Hopefully you'll be the kind of manager who can build teams people will enjoy being on.

Building Your Team With Activities That Won't Suck: A Team Building Activity

For this activity, make three lists as pictured below. **List One** should detail all activities your company and/or team do that either add value to team dynamics/productivity (green column), or are enjoyable with no workflow impact (yellow column), or are clearly not enjoyable (red column). If you are unsure how your team feels about these activities, send out an anonymous survey!

In **List Two**, write down the problems on your team that need solved, possible solutions, and an activity that can leverage full team participation to solve the problem. Columns two and three just made you start to sweat, didn't they? The good news is that you don't actually have to come up with these by yourself. You can gather the team together to hear their ideas, and then (guess what?) they are engaged in team building!

Finally, in **List Three**, write down everything you thought you had communicated clearly to your team but was actually misunderstood. If you are having trouble with this one, your team can help you out! Brace yourself. You don't want to be defensive, react in hurt or anger, or go radio silent on them. Be there to "hear," to learn, and to change. Engaging your team in this way will help to break down obstacles to collaboration and communication. There is no "one size fits all" when it comes to things that will or will not work for your team, and who better to assess that than you and your team! Remember to "keep it fun!"

Team Building Activity		
List One: **Activities your team does for "fun"**		
Add to team dynamics & productivity	Enjoyable, with no impact to workflow	Clearly not enjoyable
List Two: **Problems, solutions and collaboration**		
Problem(s) on Your Team	Possible Solutions or Fixes	Activity to Solve Problem(s)
List Three: **Everything you communicated to your team but were misunderstood about**		
What barriers did you identify?		
How did you overcome the barriers?		
What can you do to create boundaries?		
How can you increase encouragement?		
How can you inspire your team?		
How will you increase listening?		

COMMUNICATION STRATEGIES

KEEP YOUR TEAM ALIGNED

The Issue

Communication is something humans do all the time, and we're pretty good at it. However, when you are a manager, "pretty good" is not enough. How your department performs is crucially dependent on how well you communicate to employees (AND how well you listen to them). There is a lot that needs to be said and heard in your busy days, so you need to become a master of communication.

A Short Story

Alysha and Robert were happy. They'd worked all weekend to create their presentation on a sustainability issue, and it was damn convincing. It was a topic they had been researching for weeks; one of those projects they could really put heart and soul into.

Key Terms and Definitions

Listening to Understand – To listen with the intent of understanding the other's position, rather than listening only to enable you to make your next point.

Inference – A kind of educated guess rather than direct evidence.

192

HR Fundamentals for Non-HR Managers: Can We Be Friends? (& CYA!)

The project began after the CEO had made a public statement that the company was going to become greener, for example, by reducing the use of harmful chemicals. Since Alysha and Robert were chemical engineers, their boss, the VP of Manufacturing, had tasked them with making a proposal.

It wasn't easy coming up with the process changes that would have a significant impact on the use of chemicals, but the two engineers had put their heads together and come up with some great ideas. Now they were going to present their ideas to their boss, and once they got the green light, take it to the CEO.

During the presentation, their boss looked...(what was it?)...a little distracted. At the end, he said, "Nice, nice...but, um, do you have anything in there on reducing greenhouse gas emissions?"

Alysha said, "No, not really, no. The project was to reduce the use of harmful chemicals."

Partner with HR (and CYA)

It really helps with HR's communications if you have occasional one-on-one check-ins to see if employees understand key messages.

Her boss replied, "Yeah, I know, that's kind of right but actually wrong. We were originally thinking of looking at chemicals, but the leadership team decided it would be better to focus on greenhouse gas emissions instead. You need to present a report on greenhouse gases."

The appalled look on their faces cast a pall across the room.

"I told you guys they changed the topic, didn't I?" said the boss. "Sorry if I forgot to pass along that recent change."

Lost in Translation – Why Communication Matters

There is no end to the stories of those things that get "lost in translation." Sometimes, we feel that we are speaking different languages or playing the whisper game of "Telephone!" It's obvious that unclear messages lead to wasted effort. Surprisingly, the wasted effort should not be your biggest concern. Your biggest concern should be how demoralizing it is for people to find out that their work counted for nothing.

Take a moment to consider What, When and How before you blast off another email to your staff.
#ThinkBeforeSpeaking

The When

- Do people need to know this right now or would it fit in a weekly recap?

- Is this a good time to reach the person? Will they be receptive?

According to data, history, or even intuition, when is the optimal time to share this communication?

You probably spend almost six hours a day (or more) communicating. It's worth investing deliberate effort in becoming an exceptional communicator, so that those six hours of communication deliver the results you need.

Communicating – What, When & How

Average communicators will blast out emails, more concerned with just getting the communication done than whether that communication will have the desired effect. Great communicators spend just a moment reflecting on the What, When, and How of their communication.

The What

- Is this just straightforward information?

- Is this a sensitive matter?

- Am I trying to inspire people?

What, specifically, is the needed message?

194

HR Fundamentals for Non-HR Managers: Can We Be Friends? (& CYA!)

The How

- Does this need to be a conversation?
- Should this be communicated to the whole team at once in a meeting?
- Do people need a written explanation?
- Will a quick email get the outcome I need?

To accomplish your desired impact, how should you deliver your message?

You don't need to memorize this list of bullet points; just take away the main lesson. The main lesson is that you get to be a great communicator by pausing for a moment and considering the what, when, and how of each communication.

How to Do Daily Check-Ins

Most communication has some particular content you want to get across—that's why we recommend thinking about the What, When, and How. There is an important type of communication where you don't have any content to share: "The daily check-in."

Frequent two minute check-ins go a long way in enhancing communication.

It's a great idea to spend a couple of minutes every day or two doing a quick check-in with each employee. Consider asking one of these questions:

- What's your top priority right now?
- Is anything getting in the way of getting your work done?

- Is there anything I can help you with?
- What's on your mind?
- Are things going well with the team?

There are lots of things you can ask. Just stay away from, "How's it going?" because the common response to that is simply, "Fine," which won't give you any detail. Remember, a check-in isn't about saying hello; it's about getting some feedback or finding out if the employee is on track and how you can help them be more productive.

Compliance Do's and Don'ts

- Communication is good but be careful about asking people personal questions.
- For example, you shouldn't ask a woman if she is planning to have children.

Why do some managers skip this simple check-in? One common answer is that they don't have time. That's a poor answer because it's not true. Busy as they may be, they *do* have a few minutes here and there to do a quick check-in. Saying, "I don't have time" is code for, "I don't think it's that important." For managers, this is code for, "I haven't yet recognized how much poor communication hurts productivity."

Another reason managers skip check-ins is that they don't have anything they want to convey. That is almost worse than, "I don't have time." The point of a check-in isn't to convey information; it's to get it. So just go out there, ask those simple questions, and pay attention to what you find out.

Correcting Common Communication Mistakes

There are as many "how to's" on communicating as there are grains of rice in a 10-pound sack. You should cherish each tip the way a master sushi chef cherishes a grain of rice. These tips are nourishing and collectively, over time, they help you become a great communicator.

There isn't space here for thousands of tips, so instead we will just share six communications strategies most valuable for managers to practice:

- **Develop video conferencing skills.** If video conferencing is relatively new for you, you need to get good at it. For example, when you are on a video call, have the camera close to eye level. If you're using a laptop, prop it up on top of a couple of books. Use your webcam to develop a sense of presence with those you meet.

- **Edit for conciseness.** After you write the first draft, go back and delete unnecessary ideas, paragraphs, and words. This may take you a little longer, but it leads to much improved communication.

- **Always have a call to action.** At the end of any message, conversation, or meeting, it should be crystal clear to everyone what will happen next, what you as the manager commit to do, and what you are expecting them to do.

- **Really listen.** It's easy to convince ourselves we are listening well when we are only half-listening. When you are meeting with someone, give them your full attention. Don't answer an email while they are talking. Sit on your hands if that's what it takes to keep them off your phone or keyboard.

- **Be wary of a critical tone.** People are finely tuned to pick up on any criticism, so be careful with your words and tone. Watch their reaction and if there is even a little flinch, then that's an indication that what you said may have landed wrong.

- **Learn the skill of speaking clearly to people whose first language is not English.** If you are speaking to people where English is their second language, then speak each word distinctly. You understand "furgettaboutit," but they may not. (It's okay if this has happened. We all make mistakes sometimes; just learn from it.)

196

HR Fundamentals for Non-HR Managers: Can We Be Friends? (& CYA!)

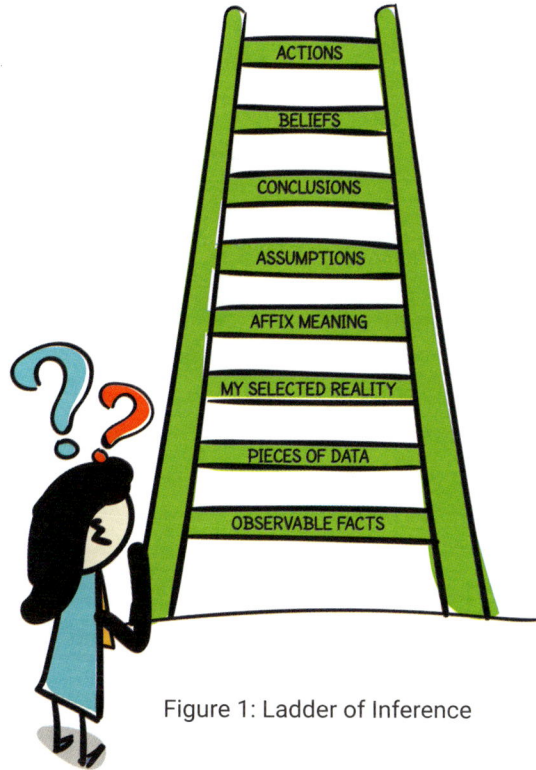

Figure 1: Ladder of Inference

Harvard Professor Chris Argyris has mapped the way we jump to conclusions in something he calls the Ladder of Inference (check out Figure 1). [53]

As described by Dr. Heidi Scott, HR.com's Chief Learning Officer,

What the diagram implies is that we begin with Observable Facts and Pieces of Data—the kind that would be captured by a movie camera without any judgments or assumptions attached.

So far so good, but as we move up to the next rung of the ladder, 'My Selected Reality,' we edit Real Data and Experience into something that may not accurately capture the full picture. And then? Well, then it might get worse. We 'Affix Meaning' to that Selected Reality, throw in Assumptions, and come to Conclusions.

As we continue climbing up the ladder, all based on a Star Trek-like voyage to the frontier, we've made up in our minds, we form beliefs (these could be about a person, that person's motivation, a system, culture, or company, etc.). Finally, based on those beliefs, we're off and running to take action. [54]

The Ladder of Inference

Have you ever had a situation where you thought you understood what someone needed, only to discover that you were completely off base? How does that happen? It turns out humans are masters of taking just the tiniest piece of information and jumping to bold conclusions (e.g. Janet changed her haircut, she must have broken up with her fiancé).

People often believe that their actions are based on data. When in fact this long ladder of inference separates data from action. In any one step up the rungs, things can go wrong. (You can learn more about the ladder of inference in *The Fifth Discipline Fieldbook* by Senge, Kleiner, Roberts, Ross, & Smith) [55]

> **Make a distinction between an observation and your inference based on the observation.**

There are a few tactics you can use to counter the natural human tendency to carelessly race up the ladder of inference:

- Get in the habit of seeking alternative explanations for an observation (e.g. Maybe the new haircut means something is wrong; maybe it means the hairdresser was giving a discount, or maybe it means she's going to attend a special event).

- Get in the habit of framing conclusions as "I wonder..." rather than as a fact (e.g. "Based on this observation, I wonder if something's wrong," rather than concluding, "Something's wrong").

- When someone makes an interpretation, ask them what evidence that is based on. In other words, try to get them to step down a few rungs on the ladder (e.g. "You say the project is bound to fail. What evidence are you basing that on?).

As the manager, those habits, combined with an awareness of the ladder of inference, will save you from many mistakes over the course of your career.

Listening Better

Why aren't all managers skilled listeners? We expect it's mainly because they have so much on their plate; it's hard to concentrate. You are going to have to work at being an engaged listener—it's not something that comes easily. Here are a few simple tactics that can help:

- **Look people in the eye.** When you are looking people in the eye, it's a lot harder to let your attention wander. It shows respect while helping you avoid the temptation to stop listening and start thinking about something else. This is especially true during a web-conference meeting. Use your cameras to increase accountability to focus on the other person "face-to-face" in the virtual setting.

> **Many successful managers are obsessive note takers.**

- **Interrupt judiciously.** It's okay to interrupt to get clarification. If you lose the thread of what someone is saying, it's hard to keep listening. Don't hesitate to interrupt and ask, "Sorry, but can you go over that point? It wasn't clear to me."

- **Take notes.** There are many advantages to taking notes, one of which is that it helps you really focus on the conversation - which makes you a better listener.

- **Repeat back what you heard.** If you plan to paraphrase back what you heard concisely, then it will force you to listen. It also is a good way to ensure the conversation stays on track and that what you think you heard is actually what they meant.

- **Train those you lead to be better talkers.** This is a listening tip you won't hear very often but it can help a lot. If employees tend to come to you with long, winding points of view, it's hard to keep listening. Give yourself a break and teach them a new skill. Tell them that you want to hear what they have to say, but you would like them to better prepare themselves first. Ask them to come back in an hour and tell you in 10 words the main point of the conversation they'd like to have. Teach them that discipline, and it will make listening a lot easier. (Be sure YOU occasionally practice this as well!) #EngageBrainBeforeMouth

Getting Input

One particular type of listening is asking for input. Many employees wish their managers would ask for their input before giving direction. As discussed in the article, *Research: Why Managers Ignore Employees' Ideas*,

> When employees share novel ideas and bring up concerns or problems,

organizations innovate and perform better.

Employees are often the first to see issues on the frontlines, so their input can really help managerial decision making.

Yet, managers do not always promote employees' ideas. In fact, they can even actively disregard employee concerns and act in ways that discourage employees from speaking up at all. [56]

Asking your team questions will give you trust "creds" with them because you are showing that you value their ideas and expertise, which demonstrates your respect for them. Just make sure you act on those ideas, or explain why you cannot implement them at this time. Otherwise, you can derail trust in a New York minute!

> Don't assume employees know the big picture. Explain why you've asked them to do a certain task.

Back to the Story

Alysha and Robert were able to "pivot" and pull together some ideas on reducing emissions of greenhouse gases, but it was far from their best work. Furthermore, they were deeply demoralized. They put their hearts into a project and then saw it wasted because of a careless lack of communication.

From the manager's perspective….well, he *thought* they knew they should be working on greenhouse gases. Certainly, the shift in focus was much discussed at his level of the organization. His approach to communication was "as needed" instead of "rigorous and consistent," which leaves lots of opportunities for things to fall through the cracks.

In this case, the manager could have easily caught the problem by using one of the basic tactics of rigorous communication: the daily check-in. If he'd only found a couple of minutes to ask Alysha or Robert what they were working on, he would have discovered right away they were off track. Let's hope the manager learned that lesson.

Summing Up

Communication takes up much of your day as a manager, being not just good at it, but great at it, will lead to better performance. There are a few key things to remember:

- Communication involves both telling and listening; you need to be great at both.

- Poor communication is common; you should learn and practice as many communication tactics as you can. Set yourself apart as a highly effective manager!

- People often jump to conclusions from scanty data by climbing the Ladder of Inference too fast. Be aware of the tendency.

- Daily check-ins are a simple way to improve team communications and really hear your people.

- It's hard to be a good listener. You'll need to intentionally work at it.

- Asking for input before giving direction is much appreciated by employees.

200

HR Fundamentals for Non-HR Managers: Can We Be Friends? (& CYA!)

Love your Idea (but no, because...):
A Team Building Activity

Now let's try an activity to see the impact of communication style.

Here's a little exercise you can do with your team to show how a slight change in approach can go from stifling a conversation to elevating it.

Start by getting your team to sit around a table, then go through three phases:

Phase 1: "No, because..."
Ask the first person to propose a place they would like to hold an offsite meeting.

Each other person in turn then responds by saying "No, because..." and comes up with a reason to shoot down that suggestion.

When they've gone through the exercise, ask the first person how they feel.

Phase 2: "Yes, but...."
This runs the same way as in Phase 1, however people respond to the suggested place of an offsite meeting with "Yes, but..."

At the end, ask the person who proposed the idea how they feel after that "Yes, but..." feedback.

Phase 3: "Yes, and..."
Finally, we repeat the exercise where people now respond to a suggestion with "Yes, and..."

The "Yes, and..." should build on or modify the original idea.

As before, ask how that felt.

The lesson is that we can promote energizing, productive communication simply by responding in a slightly different way. As a team, begin to practice using "Yes, and..." communication.

PERFORMANCE MANAGEMENT

IT'S NOT JUST ONCE A YEAR

Key Terms and Definitions

Performance Management – a process for setting and monitoring individual employee's goals; helping them improve, and planning their development.

Agile Performance Management – a performance management process that emphasizes frequent meetings to review goals and performance.

Partner with HR (and CYA)

HR hopes you don't confuse getting the forms filled out with true day-to-day performance management--but do fill in the forms (e.g. appraisals) correctly and on time.

The Issue

In a way, your whole job as a manager is about managing performance. Most organizations have a performance management process that adds a formal structure to that everyday work of getting people to perform. The formal structure has several objectives; the most important of these are to:

- Ensure there is clarity around goals
- Create a framework for a fair evaluation at year's end
- Enable a conversation about learning and development

The tricky part is that the formal process only provides a framework. It is the day-to-day work as the manager of giving direction, coaching, and feedback that actually drives performance. As a manager, you need to understand the formal and informal sides of performance management and use them together to get results.

A Short Story

Ricky was a cheerful employee. He arrived on time every day. He was willing to stay late when needed. And he was always happy to answer all of his manager's questions.

"Hey Ricky," asked his manager. "Did you get that shipment out the door yet?"

"Not yet," Ricky replied with a smile. "We're working on it."

Ricky had a creative streak and brought a wide range of responses to questions about work including: "Righty, it's in progress, so just as soon as I can get to it," "I've been fighting fires all day. Check-in with me when the smoke clears," and "We're up to our neck in alligators down here, but you're my top priority."

His manager was a bit concerned that over the course of the year, as far as he could tell, Ricky didn't get much work done. Now it was time to write up the performance appraisal form, and he wasn't clear what he should say. He certainly wasn't looking forward

Research shows organizations that excel at performance management are more likely to hold managers accountable for doing it well!

to saying anything negative to Ricky. The manager also realized that he probably should have said something about how shipments need to go out right on time. But that was back in March, so it seemed a bit late to bring it up now.

In the end, the manager simply wrote: "Meets expectations." He was still a bit concerned about explaining this, because he had a strong suspicion that Ricky was thinking he would get an "Exceeds expectations" rating. Any way you look at it, this wasn't going to be a useful meeting.

Why Performance Management is Important

Justin Reynolds in *The Importance of Ongoing Feedback in Performance Management* states:

> Employees can't reach their full potential on their own. Even someone like LeBron James has a number of coaches analyzing his approach to the game of basketball to give him pointers to help him become an even better player.
>
> Similarly, from entry-level workers to employees in senior management, all members of your team (including you!) need outside assistance to become the best they can be in their respective roles.
>
> Just like athletes are coached, business professionals can benefit tremendously from their bosses supporting them, assessing their strengths and weaknesses, and offering feedback and advice to improve performance and make sure everyone's on the same page. [57]

What you want to get out of your performance management system is:

- **Alignment on goals**: Left to their own devices, employees will work on what seems important from their vantage point. You need to ensure their goals are aligned with the bigger picture.

- **A nudge:** Most people need a little push and a clear goal to reach optimal productivity. You can set achievable targets and hold them accountable for reaching those targets.

- **Problem-solving and learning:** It's not usually described this way, but one of the things you want out of performance management is the opportunity to help employees solve problems and learn so that they will get better at achieving goals.

- **A fair and acceptable way of making pay decisions:** It's always hard to make decisions about performance ratings and pay, however without some system it is impossible to justify your decisions to the employees or your manager.

- **A thoughtful plan for each employee's development.** At least once a year, managers need to spend some time with employees to reflect on their developmental goals and needs, and to discover where they want to go in their career.

204

HR Fundamentals for Non-HR Managers: Can We Be Friends? (& CYA!)

A mix of the formal process and informal day-to-day actions will help you achieve these important outcomes.

The Common Problems of Performance Management

We can probably all agree that an annual performance review is typically dreaded by both the manager and the employee. Root canals, anyone? In fact, only 30% of managers say their performance management system is effective or very effective at helping meet organizational goals. [58]

When conducting annual reviews, have you heard any of these responses?

- "Last February?! I wish you had pointed this out to me then!"

- "Why did I omit that step? I barely remember that project, except that we were in a time crunch and we were all working double overtime to get it done."

- "Three of the targets on our plan were for projects that we canceled, and we never set any targets for the new project so how can you assign a rating?"

All of these issues stem from treating performance management as a once-a-year event. You need to be giving feedback frequently, and you probably need to review goals and targets quarterly. Your mission is to ensure that by year-end the employee already knows exactly what will be in the annual appraisal. They'll know what targets they achieved, which ones they missed, mistakes they made, and successes you applauded. This is something you can do as a manager irrespective of the performance management system your organization has in place.

The discipline of doing continuous performance management doesn't come naturally to most people. It's a skill you'll have to learn as a manager. It's difficult because you have to be tough on employees and tell them they are falling short of expectations (which doesn't mean you don't still love them). However, most of the common problems of performance management can be largely remedied by managing performance every day all year long.

The Role of Appraisals

The main point of performance management is to improve performance. (We know it seems crazy to have to keep saying this, but too often the main point of performance management is thought to be filling in a form.) Unfortunately, sometimes the goal of improving performance is overshadowed by the goal of coming up with an appraisal that will affect pay and potential promotions.

While it may seem that improving performance and making an appraisal are closely aligned (e.g. it's all about setting goals and targets), in practice there is quite a different feel about these two things. One is about helping; the other is about judging.

You need to keep these two aspects separate in your mind even if they appear together in the same sentence, "Love how you are improving your presentations by including more data, but you're still not quite at the point of meeting expectations." Yes, that's the old velvet glove followed by the iron fist. Remember, you need both; don't let one eclipse the other.

Agile Performance Management

Over the past few years, pretty much everyone has come to recognize that running performance management as a once-a-year meeting isn't effective. People have started talking about "Agile" performance management to describe an approach that has more frequent check-ins and is generally 'lighter' without so much emphasis on filling in forms.

The term agile comes from software development. Software development suffered from long-drawn-out processes where problems weren't discovered until the very end when the software was delivered. Agile software development works in short cycles where the team creates something a user can react to and then corrects course based on the feedback. The idea is that if you are

going to fail, you should "fail fast" so that you can recover.

Agile performance management has the same approach to quickly identify the "fails" so they can be turned into "sails!" #SmoothSailingAhead

Here's BambooHR's take on an agile approach to performance management:

Within a typical performance management system, managers are responsible for tracking and developing performance with their own team members and then reporting to the higher leadership team. In the past, the performance management process often consisted of a round of annual performance reviews for each employee. However, as research reveals the effectiveness of frequent feedback more and more, many companies have dropped the annual review model and adopted a system of regular manager check-ins and informal feedback sessions. This type of performance management can help employees understand

and align with company goals and objectives regularly, making small adjustments over time instead of trying for one larger course correction at the end of every year. [59]

Objectives and Key Results (OKRs)

Agile performance management includes an approach called "Objectives and Key Results" (OKRs) to set and measure priorities. It typically runs on a quarterly cycle. It makes a distinction between an "Objective" which is a lofty goal (e.g. "We aim to have the cheapest and easiest to use product on the market") and "Key Results" which are highly specific and measurable (e.g. "The design specs will improve customer net promoter score by 5% by March 11th"). The objective reminds the employee what they are aiming for; the key result tells them how their progress is measured.

In an OKR system, success on Key Results is not directly tied to the appraisal. This allows people to tackle projects where it's hard to know what the right target is and encourages them to set ambitious key results. No doubt someone who never achieves their key results is less likely to get a high appraisal than someone who always does, but there is a good dose of managerial judgment so that the person setting ambitious goals is not penalized over the person who sets easy ones.

OKRs are shared across the organization. Any employee can see any other employee's (or their manager's) objectives and key results. This transparency can aid communication (it also helps avoid that dreaded situation where two people are independently working on the same thing).

No performance management system is easy. It takes experience to learn to set the right key results. It takes discipline to review and update these monthly. It takes wisdom to identify the few key results that should be emphasized versus the many other things an employee has to do. So what's the upside? The upside is improved performance. Many top companies swear by the effectiveness of their OKR process.

Conversations Are at the Heart of Agility

There is the formal process of setting goals or key results and then there is the continuous work of actually improving performance. That work is, in fact, nothing more or less than many conversations.

Conversations help team members align their work with top-level objectives. David Hassell explains in his article, *5 Lessons To Align Your Team and Achieve Astronomical Results*,

> "Continual communications help individuals understand where they fit in the big picture, and helps them prioritize tasks to line up with the company's greater mission." [60]

Don't walk away thinking "I just have to have conversations? Piece of cake!" Research shows that only 29% of HR professionals agree that managers are good at having conversations with employees about performance. [61] If you want to be among that 29%, you'll have to work at it.

Here are three regular types of conversation typically found in agile performance management:

Incremental Communication Meetings: These happen at regular intervals, either in stand-ups (keep them short and simple!) or through brief video-conferencing, so that each person's updates can be shared. This is vital for pinpointing where to pivot if necessary, or, in a team, it facilitates collaboration. Completed tasks are discussed and any obstacles are shared. Sometimes these have dependencies. As the manager, you can inspire creative solutions to any "stucks." #GooBeGone

Ongoing Check-ins: These could be a weekly or monthly informal review of top priorities. It's a chance for the manager and employee to share ideas on the current status and solve any problems so that they can move forward.

Objective Retrospective: (Say THAT three times fast!) Agile methodology promotes ongoing reflection to help individuals and teams learn from their wins and mistakes, but more importantly, ensures that their time is continually spent on the most important goals. When priorities, initiatives, or projects have gained some momentum (perhaps quarterly?), each team member will analyze the progress made against the objectives, recount the benchmarks met, review derailments and achievements, and create a successful path to completion. Whoa, progress is on steroids, now! They can also recommend that an objective be tabled or discarded. Homestretch! This is an excellent time to recognize individual and/or team achievements. #PartyTime [62]

Diagnosing Why People are Not Performing

Your goal-setting process should have people pointed in the right direction, but what if they are still not performing? Take a moment just to think of the reasons you think employees do not perform. What is top of mind?

A useful approach for diagnosing why an individual is not performing is to ask which of these three factors might be missing: skill, motive, or opportunity:

- **Skill**: Maybe the employee doesn't have the skills to do the job. If that's the case, then you need to find a way to help them learn the skill or find someone else to do the job.

- **Motive**: Maybe the person isn't motivated to do the work. It may be a type of work they don't like. It might be that the incentive system is rewarding them for working on something else. It might be that they are just not a hard worker. If motivation is the issue, then that's what you need to address—and remember different people are motivated by different things, so use an approach crafted to that individual.

- **Opportunity**: Maybe the person doesn't have the opportunity to do the work, for example, they are on five other high priority projects and simply cannot find time to work on the goal you set. If this is the case, you have to create an opportunity for them to do the work.

The reason this simple framework is so useful is that we tend to jump to one explanation ("That guy is lazy") when it could be any one of the three. Do this quick performance diagnosis before jumping in with a performance solution.

> **When giving feedback, focus on the behavior not someone's personality.**

Giving Feedback

Many of the conversations you have in agile performance management will involve giving feedback. Feedback is, of course, a good thing. Justin Reynolds in *The Importance of Ongoing Feedback in Performance Management* identifies the following advantages of ongoing feedback in performance management which include:

- improves productivity
- builds strong relationships
- keeps employees engaged
- increases employee retention
- eliminates surprises during review time

- helps introverted employees learn new skills
- teaches coaches something, too
- encourages new ideas [63]

Here are some tips for giving feedback that are suggested in Clear Company's *Giving Effective Performance Feedback: A Guide for Managers* and adapted here:

1 Focus on the behavior, not the person

When managers are delivering feedback focused on improvement, it needs to be seen as actionable and supported by facts. Feedback should always be about the behavior, not the employee or their intentions. For instance, an effective approach for managers to address an employee's behavior can go as followed: "I've noticed that you've arrived late to our weekly meetings twice this month." A non-effective way would be stating, "You have been very inconsiderate." For feedback to have real value, it needs to be supported by concrete evidence and not just opinion.

2 Provide consistent and frequent positive feedback

82% of employees appreciate feedback, whether it's positive or negative. Nobody likes being in the dark, right? When positive feedback is delivered more frequently than negative, your employees will be open to receiving constructive guidance more often. Before providing negative feedback, examine and address the actions the employee took that got them to this point and define future positive steps for performance improvement. Remember to focus more often on the positive. Because who likes a "Negative Nelly?!"

❸ Ensure that feedback is ongoing and consistent

Managers who provide consistent feedback ensure roadblocks do not occur or that poor work isn't repeated. And employees agree, with 96% saying that receiving feedback regularly is a good thing. Employee feedback can be quick and easy (no, really it can!). Managers would be wise to give ongoing and consistent feedback instead of waiting until full performance reviews happen. Three cheers for "agile performance management!"

❹ Offer opportunities for development

Part of performance feedback is showcasing areas for employee improvement, as well as areas for growth and development. Developmental guidance should always be actionable and draw on the individual's strengths. To deliver guidance, build an ongoing plan that supports their career development. #SuperHeroesEverywhere

❺ Celebrating Success

Celebrating important milestones injects life into an organization, making it worthwhile for employees; celebrate good times - come on! (You know you're gonna hum that all day long now!) About 78% of employees said that being recognized motivates them in their job. Managers need to praise and celebrate the success of each of their employees. Not only does this boost performance, but it reinforces that employees are valued throughout your organization.[64]

Back to the Story

Cheerful Ricky wasn't performing well. Whose fault was that? The grasshopper in the Disney movie *Antz* has the answer, "The first rule of leadership: everything is your fault." Maybe Ricky didn't have the clear key results he needed to keep him on track. Maybe he was missing some skills he needed to develop. Perhaps he didn't feel motivated to get things finished on time. Whatever the problem was, it was his manager's responsibility to find out and fix. A well-executed performance management process with the structure of clear goals backed by ongoing conversations would get Ricky on track.

Ricky's manager looked at the appraisal form. He knew that this year it was far too late to fix things. He decided to spend the appraisal meeting talking with Ricky about how they should approach performance next year.

Summing Up

Why is the organization paying you to be a manager? It's because they expect you to improve your team's performance. The performance management process, both the formal part that involves filling in forms and the informal day-to-day conversations about performance, is an important tool for improving team performance.

Here are some of the key ideas:

- Many managers struggle with performance management, and while it is never easy, it will be effective if you do it right.

- The key to doing it right is having ongoing conversations and occasional structured meetings—not just a single annual performance management meeting.

- Keep the ideas of helping an employee improve and appraising an employee separate in your mind. They are closely related, but have a very different emotional tone.

- Diagnose why an employee is not performing before jumping in with a solution like training.

- Managers need to be skilled at giving feedback, develop this skill.

Good managers spend their whole career getting ever better at improving their team's performance in all kinds of different situations. Embrace this journey.

Create a Continual, Positive Feedback Environment: A Team Building Activity

Whatever your company has asked you to measure could be what they value most, but how each of your team members will be assessed may not reflect this. For this activity, assemble a focus group from your current team. (Remember to include unlikely suspects!) Ask them to make a list of short term goals related to:

- activities and tasks that they do,

- which tasks are quantifiable, and

- which tasks are time-sensitive.

Ideally, work to ensure that the team remains aware of the company's goals. This will aid in aligning the team members' short and long term goals with where the company is going. It also increases the amount of meaningful work that team members are doing.

Next, for the long term goals (this will be WAY trickier!), have them think about activities and tasks that do not produce immediate results but will "pay off" over time.

- What kind of results are required?

- Within what reasonable timeframes?

- What are some ideas on how to measure efficacy?

As the manager, you may feel you have to come up with these things on your own. However, don't forget that being a team coach means that you can trust your team and their input. Optimizing any process should be a collaboration and not a "top-down" venture. The rewards? They are endless, provided you keep engaging others for their input! #NoLoneRangersAllowed

Team Focus Group					
Short-Term Goals			Long-Term Goals		
Activities & Tasks	Quantifiable Tasks	Time-sensitive Tasks	Results Desired	Results Timeframe	How to Measure Success

SECTION 8

Retention and Mobility:
Making all the right moves

RETENTION

KEEPING YOUR EMPLOYEES FROM EXITING STAGE LEFT

Key Terms and Definitions

Turnover – **the number of employees who leave in one year as a percentage of the employee population.**

Retention – **How long employees stay on average with your company.**

The Issue

Every time an employee quits, it creates a cascade of costs. There are the costs of hiring and training. There is the cost of lower team performance while the job is vacant. There is the cost of the new hire getting up to speed. Often there is knowledge or customer relationships that can be diminished or lost and not easily replaced. Finally, there are costs for the time and effort you as a manager need to put into dealing with the disruption.

There are various rules of thumb for estimating the cost of turnover. Here's one:

> ...replacing a mid-level employee can cost 20 percent of their annual salary, meaning a $60,000 per year manager can cost about $12,000 to replace. Meanwhile, replacing a high-level employee, with large salaries and specialized training, can cost up to 213 percent of their salary. This puts the direct cost of replacing a $100,000 per year C-Suite Executive at up to $213,000. [65]

One thing that all turnover cost estimates have in common: they are always high. Retention is an important issue for all managers.

214

HR Fundamentals for Non-HR Managers: Can We Be Friends? (& CYA!)

Partner with HR (and CYA)

HR wants you to recognize that your behavior is the single biggest reason employees leave or stay.

A Short Story

Mambo was coming up to the age when he would be eligible for early retirement and his boss, Ali, knew him well enough that he was pretty sure he would take it. Ali was happy for Mambo, but it left him with a problem. Who could take over Mambo's role?

Ali considered the options for his replacement. The employee he kept coming back to in his mind was Jerome. It would be a big step up for Jerome, but Ali felt sure he could do it. Ali had always secretly considered Jerome a high potential employee. He had the smarts and the drive to take on new challenges.

The more Ali thought about it, the more he liked the idea. After all, Jerome had been in the same role for six years. He was bound to be ready for a change. Furthermore, the tight budget meant that Jerome hadn't had a significant raise in

years, and his promotion would lead to a handsome increase in salary. All in all, it was a win-win situation. Ali would have a great replacement for Mambo, and Jerome would have a well-deserved promotion. Perfecto!

Meanwhile, unbeknownst to Ali, Jerome had been thinking something similar. He had indeed been in the same role for six years and hadn't received a significant raise in some time. Ali had never discussed his career or potential advancement, so he was pretty sure he would be stuck in the same role for life. That's why he was on the phone with a headhunter. All in all, it was a win-win the headhunter assured him. Jerome would be a great hire for the competitor, and he would receive a well-deserved promotion. Perfecto!

Jerome was ready to accept an external offer on the spot.

Avoidable and Regrettable Turnover

Turnover is a major issue for most organizations. By some estimates, $11 billion is lost in the United States each year due to unnecessary turnover. [66]

HR departments often make a distinction between avoidable and unavoidable turnover. Retirement, death, going back to school, and moving out of town are all causes of unavoidable turnover.

Sometimes HR also uses the term "regrettable turnover." In essence, this excludes low performers. We don't regret it when a low performer leaves our organization.

> ## Not all turnover is bad.

As a manager, you are concerned with avoidable, regrettable turnover. If there are good people you wanted to keep, and could have kept but they left, then that's an expensive problem you'll want to fix.

Why Employees Leave

Why do employees leave a job? Why would they leave your team in particular? The answers are not mysterious. They think the job is crappy. Lousy jobs are so common they have their own day according to Hillary Wright's article,

> March 31, 2016 was "International Quit Your Crappy Job Day," a holiday of sorts, declared by Woohoo Inc. (a Danish management training firm), on behalf of an estimated 20-25 percent of employees who hate their jobs and wish they could quit tomorrow. [67]

We should be a little more specific in our analysis of reasons. Why is the job crappy? A common reason is that employees don't like their boss. CNBC/SurveyMonkey Workplace

Happiness Index: July 2019 found that 49% of workers are not satisfied with their direct supervisor. [68] Yes, that's a tough one to hear. Don't take it too hard. It doesn't mean they hate you, just that in your role as manager they felt you were not doing enough to make the job worth their time. If it is about your skill as a manager, then it means the turnover is avoidable. That's good because it's something you have some control over. Let's look at what you can do.

Engagement Surveys, Exit Interviews, and Water Coolers

A good place to start your efforts to improve retention is with data. Chances are that your HR department is already gathering engagement and exit interview data—you just need to use it. If they are not gathering this information, then ask them to help you to do so. Engagement surveys can be big projects, but they don't need to be. If your goal is to get a temperature check on the mood of your team and some insight on their priorities, then HR can send out a simple set of questions with a free survey tool.

Reason for quitting

Exit interviews are notoriously hard to do, because departing employees typically give the polite answer that they went elsewhere for more money, without revealing the true reasons they left. If HR has the skill and time to dig deeper, then they can get good insights and provide you with helpful feedback. If you can't get good exit interviews done, then use an exit survey. The answers to the survey may not provide deep insights but some data is better than no data. The exit survey can ask if any of the common reasons for leaving apply. For example, was it that they:

- Didn't like the job itself?
- Didn't get along with the team?
- Didn't get along with the manager?
- Felt lack of appreciation?
- Had too few opportunities for learning and advancement?
- Went back to school?
- Or another reason? (Ask them to explain)

One tip...the best practice is to have the interview or survey done by an outside consultant. When questions about leaving are asked by a neutral party, data shows that up to 63% of the answers will change. [69]

Another source of insight is the proverbial water cooler. (Does anyone have these anymore? Did they used to be a fixture in every workplace? We sure talk about them as if they were.) Today the virtual water cooler talk exists... you just often can't readily see where and when it takes place! Talk to your employees about how they feel about the work and workplace. Ask them how other people feel.

Once you have a sense of the likely causes of turnover, you are in a position to focus your efforts to reduce those causes.

How to Retain Good Employees

Hopefully, you've gathered some data on why employees leave or stay. While we don't have that specific data on your workplace, we do have some general tips for you. Maybe we can start with the simplest tip of all, which is that if you pay attention to your employees with the intention of treating them well, the rest may follow naturally. You may not need to read anything about the theory of retention because you'll instinctively do the right things. Nevertheless, we still can't resist sharing our other top tips:

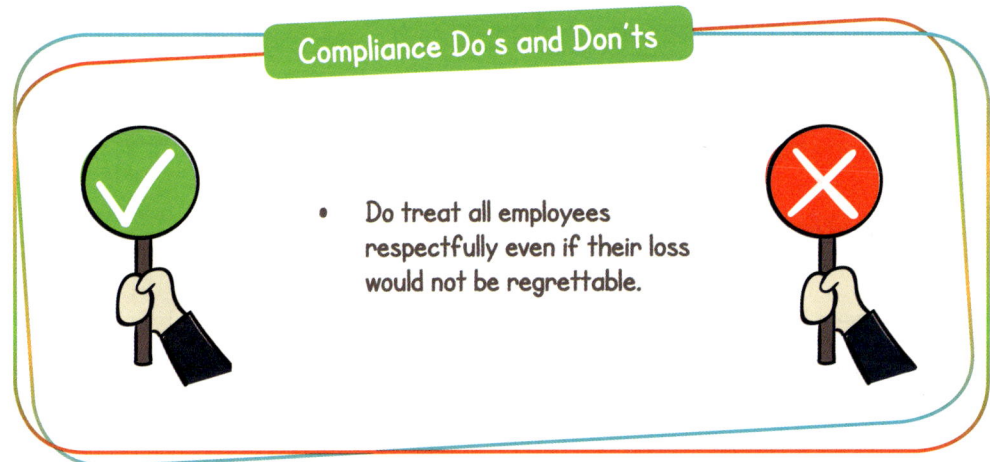

Compliance Do's and Don'ts

- Do treat all employees respectfully even if their loss would not be regrettable.

- **Show appreciation for employees' accomplishments, even small ones.** In their book, *Leading with Gratitude*, Adrian Gostick and Chester Elton point to research that one of the top reasons employees resent their manager was failing to give credit where credit was due. [70]

- **Give clear direction and show why the employee's goals matter to the organization's mission**. Employees want to know what they should do and why it matters. Take the time to do that and develop the skill to do it well.

- **Create a sense of belonging**. We've talked a lot about inclusion and if we turn from HR-speak into everyday language that means people want to like their teammates and be liked in return. In their book, *The Why of Work*, Wendy and Dave Ulrich point out that people don't need to be part of an organization that has a noble mission to make their work meaningful. Sometimes it's simply the people you work with that give you a reason to happily show up every day. [71]

- **Create opportunities to learn and develop**. Most people love to learn new things. For many younger people, learning is the main thing they want out of the workplace. Make an effort to find projects where people can develop. Let them take time off to go to meet-ups or other learning events. Talk to them about their interests and find ways to allow them to pursue those interests.

- **Assign tasks so that people do the work they are most suited for.** In his book, *The One Thing You Need to Know*, Marcus Buckingham points out that the biggest

> Give people the tasks they enjoy doing.

difference between great managers and average ones is that great managers organize work so that employees can do the things they are best at. If an employee hates detailed work, do you keep giving it to them because "they've got to learn"? You are better off giving that work to someone who enjoys it and then find other tasks that fit the employee's strengths. [72]

Retention isn't a magic trick. It's a set of everyday practices that makes your workplace a desirable one.

The Stay Interview

We've talked about the exit interview. Have you ever heard about the stay interview? The stay interview is a simple idea. Instead of waiting until an employee leaves and asking them what went wrong, you talk to an employee *while they are still an employee!* You don't have to ask the painful question, "Why did you leave me?" Instead you can ask, "What sorts of things will make you want to stay?"

218

HR Fundamentals for Non-HR Managers: Can We Be Friends? (& CYA!)

You may worry that the employee will say that what will make them want to stay is a Mercedes-Benz (after all they'll explain that their friends all drive Porsches). Don't worry as that sort of thing doesn't happen very often. Most employees are reasonable. Just ask them what they like about the job, what they'd like to do more of, what they'd like to do less of, what their interests are, or what their ambitions are. This is a relaxed chat, something that should be enjoyable for both of you. It will also arm you with the insight you need to create an environment that will make that employee want to stay.

Hiring for Retention

If you are in a role where there is naturally a lot of turnover and hence a lot of hiring, then you should ask HR to help you do a better job of hiring to improve retention. In fact, one of the common measures to determine the value of assessment tests is whether they reduce turnover. There is a whole science of assessing candidates to see if they are the type that is likely to stick around or not. Ask HR to help you with this, and with the right tools and

Hire people who are likely to stay.

processes, you can make a significant reduction in turnover just by hiring the right kinds of people.

What to Do About Unavoidable Turnover

At the start of this chapter, we suggested you focus on avoidable, regrettable turnover. What should you do about unavoidable turnover? Many industries do have high, unavoidable turnover and they get by. How do they do it?

There are just a few things to put in place:

- **Have an ongoing recruitment process; don't wait until there is a vacancy to submit a job requisition.** You can work with the recruiting

department on this. If you can forecast that you'll likely be hiring two to three people for a role each month (or whatever that number is), then the recruiting team can design their processes so that they always have candidates in the pipeline.

- **Invest extra effort in having an efficient onboarding process.** If you are doing a lot of onboarding, then you'll want the process to be effective and efficient. There are many useful software tools that help with onboarding. Again, go to HR for help.

- **Develop a knowledge transfer/ continuity management process for when people leave.** Sometimes a person leaves and they are the only one who knows where certain files are, what the password to a database is, or what the status of a client's project is. If you have high unavoidable turnover, invest in developing a standard knowledge transfer process that will ensure this basic information is not lost when the person walks out the door.

> **Don't let people walk out the door without passing on crucial knowledge.**

There is one other thing you might consider although it's harder and may not be practical in your case. There may be ways to design the work so that it's easy for new hires to be productive right away. Fast food restaurants often have work so systematized and automated that they thrive even with astonishingly high turnover.

Back to the Story

Ali got a lucky break. Jerome was all ready to accept an offer from a competitor and confidentially asked a colleague for advice. The colleague, who knew that Jerome was held in high regard, suggested he speak to Ali and mention that he'd been approached by a headhunter.

You can imagine Ali's reaction. He immediately told Jerome how he was considered a high potential employee and that he could guarantee a big promotion in the next year. He told Jerome how much he was valued and how much he personally appreciated all of the great work he had done for the team. (Too bad Ali had not conveyed his appreciation much sooner!)

Jerome was left wondering why he was never told of any of this before. Still, he knew Ali was a man of his word and turned down the competitor's offer. We hope Ali learned a lesson in management so that he wouldn't be counting on luck to retain his other star employees.

Summing Up

Retention is a metric you should be managing. Here are the key ideas we covered:

- You'll want to distinguish between avoidable and unavoidable turnover, and between regrettable and non-regrettable turnover.

- One of the most common reasons employees leave is because they don't like their boss. This means it's something you have significant control over.

- You should gather data to get insights on why people might leave; engagement surveys and exit interviews can provide this data. Also, pay attention to cues you pick up in conversations around the office or virtual water cooler.

- The overarching tip for improving retention is to pay attention to your employees and find ways to make their life at work more fulfilling.

- If high turnover is natural for your industry, work with HR to adjust hiring practices so that you select people who are likely to stay.

- When turnover is unavoidable, then invest in measures to minimize the disruption it causes.

Get retention right and you'll improve your team's effectiveness. Now let's do a tasty exercise.

The Stay for Pizza Interview

This exercise is an easy one. To the employees, it might just feel like a free pizza lunch. But to you, it's an effective tool for retention. Tell your team that you want some feedback on what makes for a happy workplace and that you'll pay them in pizza.

For your virtual team members, provide an online gift certificate for a pizza or sub-sandwich chain they have access to in their area. Of course they don't have to use it during your team lunch if it is not convenient for them. It is really the thoughtful gesture you provide that promotes the importance of this team meeting and the value they bring to the group.

Over lunch (virtual or face-to-face), in a group of 4 or 5 people, sit together over pizza and lead a discussion about the workplace. (If you have a large number of direct reports then you get to have a lot of pizza lunches ... lucky you!)

Don't ask people for their personal views the way you might in a stay interview. Instead, lead a casual discussion by asking some of the following questions:

- What do people like about working here?
- Are people happy with their chances to learn and grow?
- What do people complain about that you think is a legitimate concern?
- What could we do to make this a better workplace?
- What is great about it already?

You can let the discussion flow naturally—but take notes! In the end, be sure to practice your appreciation skills by sincerely thanking people and being specific about something each person said that you found valuable—even if some of the information shared was hard to hear.

Once you have had your meetings, go over your notes and brainstorm with your boss or HR on how to take some of the points raised in the discussions and take actions that will improve retention.

MANAGING MOVEMENT

EMPLOYEE TRANSITIONS SIDEWAYS, UPWARDS, OUTWARD

> Leaders notice managers who develop employees who can be promoted

Key Terms and Definitions

Promotion – vertical movement up the organization.

Promotion-in-place – a promotion with a new title and possibly slightly more complex duties while staying in the same role

The Issue

There can be a lot of movement between jobs in an organization. People are promoted, fired, or moved laterally. You have a role in making sure those moves go smoothly.

Let's face up to the fact that you may not want people to move out of your team. Promotion to another department is great for the employee, but it leaves you without a high performer. Put aside that short-term self-interest and consider what's good for the individual and the organization. Here's the good news; leaders notice managers who develop talent. Your skill at moving people up and laterally will be recognized and will mark you as someone who should be moved up themselves.

222

HR Fundamentals for Non-HR Managers: Can We Be Friends? (& CYA!)

Partner with HR (and CYA)

Help your good performers move laterally and vertically in the organization; don't try to keep them all to yourself.

A Short Story

Wes was very happy with David's performance as an accounting clerk. He was the best worker on the accounting team: reliable, fast, and detail oriented. David had, in many ways, earned a promotion. Unfortunately, he was already a senior clerk. There was no step up for David, other than to Wes's job of accounting manager—and Wes wasn't leaving anytime soon. That was when Wes had a brilliant idea.

Wes called David into his office. "David, you're the best clerk we've got and I don't want you to think I haven't noticed. I've decided to reward your excellent service by designating you Assistant Manager. You'll still report to me but you'll get some experience guiding the team."

David was thrilled. "I'm honored sir. I won't disappoint you. This is a big job but I can assure you I'm ready for it. Stand back! UNLEASH the Assistant Manager!"

The next Monday morning when Wes came in, he noticed that something looked different. What was it? Oh, it was that there was now a chandelier hanging over David's cubicle. Wes inquired about that and David responded that given the importance of the position of Assistant Manager it was only right to signal the change with a minor office upgrade. Wes wondered how he'd explain that expense—well, he was the accounting manager—he'd bury it somehow.

On Tuesday when Wes arrived, the office was abuzz. Everyone was looking out the window at the parking lot. Not so much the parking lot per se, as at David's new Tesla. Later on, David told Wes that though it was an expensive car, he was sure he could afford it now that he'd been promoted to Assistant Manager. Wes wondered if he'd mentioned there was no pay increase with the promotion—perhaps that had slipped his mind.

On Wednesday, Wes asked David for the quarterly report.

"Oh, the Assistant Manager can't be spending time on such trivia," David explained. "I asked one of my staff to do it. I'll go yell at her now."

It was still only Wednesday; Wes wasn't looking forward to the rest of the week. He'd unleashed a monster, and now he was going to have to find a way to reel him in.

> **Internal promotions have a higher success rate than external hires.**

Internal Moves Rather than External Hires

Often when a position opens up, managers are tempted to hire externally rather than promote or transfer from within. It's a type of the "grass is greener on the other side" syndrome. The fact is that hiring externally is expensive, and the risk of failure is higher. If you do feel that you need an external hire, you should second guess yourself as to whether that is really necessary.

Promoting from internal sources doesn't just save the company money. It shows employees that there *are* career paths that will lead to upward mobility. Promoting from within is a way to improve retention.

Promotions

Ideally, a promotion is to a new job reporting to a new manager along with a nice pay increase. For example, it's the senior barista being moved to another cafe and promoted to cafe manager. Those situations are simple. Congratulations are in order! Yes, in part for the employee promoted, but mainly for you because you did a great job developing the talent the organization needs. Buy yourself a bottle of champagne.

Many promotions are not so dramatic. They are "promotions in place" where you have the same manager, you sit at the same desk, and you mainly do the same things but with some additional responsibilities along with a small pay increase. It's the junior accounting clerk being moved up to accounting clerk or the compensation analyst being made the senior compensation analyst.

Often the decision to give a promotion in place is largely up to you as a department manager (although you will need to get approval). Sometimes you can create a "senior" role to reward and retain an employee even if that designation didn't exist in the past. This is something you'll want to discuss with your boss and then HR. There may be strict rules around giving a promotion in place or quite a bit of flexibility; you need to learn the rules in your organization.

224

HR Fundamentals for Non-HR Managers: Can We Be Friends? (& CYA!)

> **Whatever the type of promotion, make sure the expectations for the new role are made clear.**

The most important thing about promotions in place is that the employee understands exactly what it is and doesn't confuse it with the idea that they are moving to a new, bigger role. Explain to them that the company recognizes that they are now performing at a higher level and taking on more complex work. You could also explain that the company feels this should be recognized with a new title (and hopefully) pay increase. That's good—people appreciate that. Simply work to ensure their expectations match the reality. The reality is that their job tomorrow is going to feel much like their job today.

There is one ugly option that sits between a classic promotion and a promotion in place. That ugly option is to create a new (we're tempted to say "fake") level in the hierarchy so that the person thinks they're getting a real promotion. For example, you have a team of say eight people reporting to you and you promote one to be the assistant manager. Now you have the dreaded one over one organizational structure where you have just one person reporting to you. This is almost always a bad structure. Your job and their job have so much overlap in apparent responsibilities that it leads to frustration and confusion. Managers love to create these fake levels, so it happens all the time. It's still a bad idea. Don't do it.

Lateral Transfers

There are only so many roles up the hierarchy which means many employees won't have a chance to move up. What they can do is move laterally. This is good for them and good for the company. It's not so good for you because you may lose a talented employee to another department, but it's a time when you need to keep the greater good in mind.

Your role in lateral transfers is to make them possible for your team. First of all, your team should know that you want them to pursue their career interests, and you won't be angry if they mention an interest in joining another department. Secondly, recognize that your team might have no clue about what other

What to do when you can't make up but have to break up.

roles they are suited for in the company. You want to keep your eyes and ears open for them. Your career planning discussion will go a lot better if you have career options to discuss other than the fact that they could possibly get your job 20 years from now when you retire.

If you have employees whose careers you want to support, then talk to other managers about them. Let them know you've got a capable person who is probably ready to take on new challenges and that it would be great if they could find that within the organization. This isn't one of your core responsibilities; it's just a good human thing to do.

Termination

On TV, terminating employees is easy. Some jerk of a boss yells, "You're fired!" and the story moves on from there. In real life, termination is one of the most difficult things a manager has to do—and if you remain a manager for a length of time, odds are you will have

to do it. Let's get well-prepared for that inevitable challenge.

First, before you read further, please email a note to HR asking for a 15-minute call (don't mention the topic or you'll freak them out). On the call, say that while you currently have the best team ever, you are reading a book that suggests talking to HR about how termination is handled in your company. Different companies handle termination differently—and you want to gain an understanding of company processes should the day come you need to deal with this. You need to know how it is done in your organization. Ask for some stories for context (not just for policy), because sometimes (most of the time?) policy doesn't capture the reality of how termination unfolds.

There will be a difference between company mandated layoffs and letting individuals go for poor performance. It's the latter we are most interested in, because that's the one where your role is most crucial.

226

HR Fundamentals for Non-HR Managers: Can We Be Friends? (& CYA!)

> Real life isn't like TV. You can't just yell "You're fired!"

Once you are grounded in the approach your organization takes, you can consider these general principles and start applying them in your situation should you need to lay someone off for poor performance.

1 Termination shouldn't come as a surprise to the employee

It's only fair that an employee should know they are not meeting expectations. There is also a chance that if they know it's not working out, they will quit on their own, saving you the trauma of firing someone. This takes us right back to the idea of agile performance management. You want to be frequently checking in with employees as well as having more formal mid-year reviews. For low performers, you need to balance encouragement with the raw truth that as things stand, they don't meet expectations. Make sure they understand both parts of that message. It's a tough job, but, hey, no one said managing was easy.

2 You need to document everything

HR is likely to tell you that it's crucial you document everything—believe them when they tell you that. It's much harder to fire someone when their last four reviews say, "Exceeds expectations."

3 Bring HR in as your guide early on

As soon as you begin to suspect you have a low performer, begin talking to HR about how to handle the situation. The focus initially will be what you can do to bring them up to speed. Often they will ask you to create a formal "performance improvement plan." However, HR will also be painfully aware of what may need to happen months down the line if the poor performer does not turn things around. They will help you be prepared just in case this employee is unable to make the grade.

4 Be especially careful in cases that involve diversity

Is there a risk that the person you want to let go will claim it's a case of discrimination? If so, the same steps apply... just do them extra well.

5 Be compassionate

When it's time to break the news to an employee, do so in a compassionate way. If someone feels respected, listened to, and treated fairly, then they are far less likely to launch a wrongful dismissal suit. It's also simply the right thing to do. Don't forget that you need HR at this meeting.

Constructive Dismissal

What if instead of firing someone, you just treat them so badly that they leave on their own? Cool trick? NO! If you do, that is considered, under the law, to be wrongful dismissal. Now you are likely in for a lawsuit that you will lose. Don't play tricks; play it by the book and do the right thing.

Succession Planning

Let's end with a topic more upbeat than constructive dismissal. Organizations often have a process called succession planning where senior leaders and HR identify likely successors for key positions. This is in part risk management; the company will know if there are key positions it won't be able to fill easily. It is also in part a guide for training and development. If they identify someone as a possible successor who will be ready one day but is not ready yet, then they can work on developing the necessary skills so that they are ready.

Succession planning isn't easy and since it isn't urgent per se (it's about the coming years, not the coming weeks), it often is overlooked. Clifton and Harter write:

> Many companies have no succession plan at all and make these crucial decisions as needed. The absence of an organized system leads to extraordinarily high costs in external hiring. When done right, decisions to promote from within the organization result in higher success rates. This is because decision-makers can closely observe and use on-the-job performance to make better decisions. [73]

Closely related to succession planning are high potential programs. Organizations have limited resources for developing talent so they may identify some high potential employees and invest heavily in their development. If a company has developed a lot of high potentials, they may be able to readily fill key roles when they are vacant, even if they haven't developed a detailed succession plan.

Most managers are not involved in succession planning or high potential programs. They do, however, have a responsibility to develop their staff and that includes, to the extent possible, developing someone who could replace them. Some managers don't want to have anyone nearby who could replace them, but the best managers are expecting to move up themselves, and they are happy to have someone ready to step into their shoes.

Back to the Story

David had let the title of assistant manager go to his head. What Wes had created was in fact a fake promotion without thinking it through. He didn't actually want David to be managing the staff. He wanted David, as a respected and experienced employee, to provide guidance to his peers. He didn't have a budget to raise David's salary or pay for new office amenities. And on top of all that he wanted David to do the work he was doing before. There was no need for that assistant manager role.

The only solution was a quiet stroll around the building where Wes apologized for not explaining the expectations for the role. Yes, David could keep the assistant manager title and the chandelier, but the job was still that of a senior clerk. As for the Tesla, well it was a really nice car.

Summing Up

Most organizations have a fair bit of internal movement. Part of your job as a manager is helping that movement proceed smoothly. Let's review the key points in this chapter:

- It often makes more sense to transfer or promote someone internally than bring in an external hire. We sometimes fool ourselves into thinking that we'll land some remarkable candidate from the outside when in fact the internal person will be a better performer.

- There is an important distinction between a promotion that moves the employee to a new role up the hierarchy and a promotion-in-place where the person remains in (largely) the same job. Both are important, just keep the difference clear in your mind and your employee's mind.

- Lateral transfers are a productive way for your employees to develop. It's also good for the organization. Don't let the fact that you are losing a good person prevent you from supporting the move. You should even be looking for opportunities across the organization so your people can grow.

- Understand that there are many laws and policies around termination. You need to get HR involved early and you need to document everything well before you try to terminate someone.

- Organizations often have succession planning meetings to look ahead at how they might fill top jobs. Most managers need only be concerned with developing people who could fill their shoes should they move on.

Now let's tackle an activity.

Facilitating Employee Movement: An Employee Transitions Activity

If an employee is happy in their job and you are happy with their performance, then it is easy to overlook them as a candidate for a promotion or lateral move. This can lead to missed opportunities that eventually cause that employee to look for a career elsewhere.

In this activity, we ask you to look closely at three of your best employees. You should think about the careers of all employees, but for now three will be a good start.

	Employee 1	Employee 2	Employee 3
What do they have an aptitude for?			
What other jobs in the organization might they excel in with proper training?			
Which of these might be a good career move for them?			
Do you think they have the potential to move up in the organization?			
Can you give them responsibilities on a project to test your sense of their potential?			
Based on this analysis, what can you do that will move the employee a step closer to their next career move?			

SECTION 9

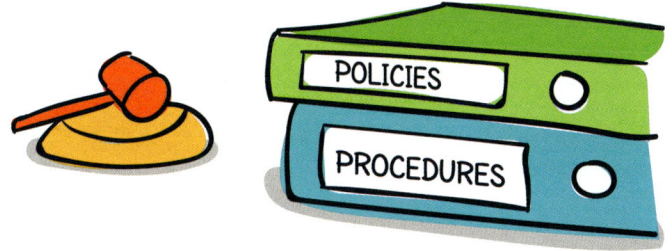

The "Love to Hate" Policies and
a Review of Core Concepts

THOSE PESKY POLICIES AND PROCEDURES

PAVING THE WAY TO COMPLIANCE

When it comes to company policies, it's best to color within the lines

Key Terms and Definitions

Policies: the formal guidelines and rules companies establish to hire, train, assess, and reward team members.

The Issue

A manager does not have nearly as much freedom as you might think. You need to comply with a significant number of policies, not to mention legislation. If you don't follow the policies, then chances are that you won't be a manager for very long.

Remember that all policies were created for a reason. Some may seem overly restrictive to you, but typically there was some circumstance that made them necessary. Often that "circumstance" is legislation. There are local, state, and federal laws that regulate the workplace. Not abiding by them can result in lawsuits against the company, and you, as an individual.

> **Partner with HR (and CYA)**

Enforce the policies and procedures.

Since you can't change the policies, you need to learn what they are and how to comply with them. You don't need to know all the details of labor legislation. Look to HR for that. But, you *do* need to avoid obvious violations and know when to ask for help. You'll also need to ensure your employees comply with the policies.

A Short Story

Jackie and her assistant, Jeff, were at a client meeting in San Francisco. The meeting went very well, thanks to Jeff's astute preparation. After the meeting, Jackie told Jeff, "You did a great job for that client. Our flight to New York isn't until late. Take the rest of the day off and relax."

Jeff, ever the loyal employee, followed his boss's instructions. He lazily strolled around Fisherman's Wharf, rode the cable car, had a relaxing (though pricey) lunch at Swan Oyster Depot, then strolled over to spend the rest of the afternoon at the Nob Hill Spa where he had a relaxing arctic berry body scrub. "Just following my boss's orders," he muttered to the massage therapist.

Next month something surprising happened. Accounting rejected his admittedly hefty expense claim. That was odd; he had all the receipts. He'd have to speak to Jackie about that! (...to be continued)

Where You Are Most Likely to Get into Trouble

If you make a mistake on a policy specific to your company, such as dress code, then you simply have to correct yourself. If it's in the policies linked to legislation—the ones where the company can be sued—you're more likely to get into significant trouble. The most prevalent areas concern equal opportunity, sexual harassment, and other forms of harassment.

Be especially alert to legislative requirements.

Equal Opportunity

The goal of the Equal Employment Opportunities Commission (EEOC) is to prevent discrimination in the workplace. You cannot discriminate on grounds of an individual's race, children, national origin, religion, sex, age, disability, sexual orientation, gender identity, or genetic information. You also can't retaliate against people for complaining about or reporting discrimination.

This all makes sense. It's why you'll find standard text in job advertisements along these lines:

> [Company Name] provides equal employment opportunities to all employees and applicants

for employment and prohibits discrimination and harassment of any type without regard to race, color, religion, age, sex, national origin, disability status, genetics, protected veteran status, sexual orientation, gender identity or expression, or any other characteristic protected by federal, state or local laws. This policy applies to all terms and conditions of employment, including recruiting, hiring, placement, promotion, termination, layoff, recall, transfer, leaves of absence, compensation and training. [74]

You may also find HR changing some of the language in one of your job postings so that it does not lean towards

COME AS YOU ARE

encouraging or discouraging one gender or other groups. It's all part of complying with equal opportunity legislation and doing the right thing.

The laws against discrimination apply broadly, including to salaries and bonuses, leave approvals, shift scheduling, and performance appraisals. You simply need to pause from time to time and ask yourself, "Am I treating everyone equally or am I letting some biases creep in?"

Equal employment opportunities legislation is most likely to affect you in interviews. As we said in the chapter on recruitment, you need to stick to the script and pay attention when HR 'kicks you under the table.'

Careful use of language will avoid discrimination.

Here is why HR and legal are so touchy about this; imagine you ask some of these questions:

So, how far was your commute to get here? (Opens up the question of where they live.)

Seemingly straightforward, no? No! If the person lives in an ethnic-centric neighborhood, you could be opening yourself up to a claim of racial discrimination. Better to ask if they have reliable transportation.

I went to ABC College, too! What year did you graduate?

Nope. This is basically asking them how old they are! Big no-no.

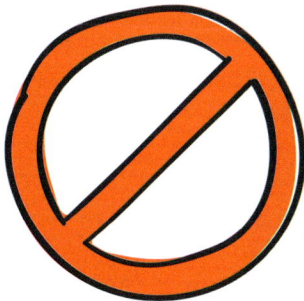

Oh, you just dropped your kids off at the XYZ Daycare? I am thinking of switching to that one, too!

This question usually comes up when chatting about daycare, first day of school, college road trips, etc. This comes up in casual conversations on the elevator, seeing a family photo on smartphone wallpaper, and other seemingly innocent contexts. But you can never let your guard down! Do not ask anything about their families.

What are your plans for the weekend?

Hobbies, caring for elderly parents, religious events … all are fodder for potential discrimination suits. At this point, you are probably thinking you will simply not talk to candidates at all!

The bottom line for you here is that you want to minimize chit-chat in interviewing so that you minimize risk. If you are sued, the judge is not going to ask you if you like the way the laws are written. You simply need to comply.

Americans with Disabilities Act (ADA)

If you follow the equal opportunity principles, then you will be treating people with disabilities fairly. In fact, the main point of the ADA is to ensure people with disabilities are not discriminated against. However, there is one extra thing you need to know about, which is the concept of "reasonable accommodation." The idea is that if someone has a disability, it's your duty to make any reasonable changes to the workplace such that they're able to do their job. For example, you may need to put in a ramp if someone in a wheelchair is unable to get to the workplace due to stairs. You may need to add some technical aids so that people with hearing, vision, or speech disabilities can communicate. When someone with a disability says, "Excuse me. I need this in order to do my job," then take that request seriously! You can't just shrug it off!

> Ignorance of the law is no excuse. (Ignorance is not bliss in this case!)

Sexual Harassment

In our current era, workplaces have adopted very strict policies around sexual harassment. Anything that might be perceived as sexual harassment is forbidden. This can be challenging for employees because it means that behaviors that might be considered innocuous outside the workplace are treated as violations inside the workplace. You have to make sure they recognize that the standards of behavior in the workplace are far higher.

Here are some of the main guidelines:

- No sexual jokes or innuendo
- No sharing or posting of sexual images
- No unnecessary touching (you can shake hands but best leave it at that)
- No repeated invitations for a date

You get the idea. Play it safe by keeping sex out of the workplace. What one person thinks is innocent, another person might consider sexual harassment. If someone gets a little out of line, then it's your job to intervene immediately. As a manager, it is also your job to communicate harassment of any kind to the HR department. If an employee files a harassment complaint with the EEOC, and you haven't communicated what was brought to your attention, you put the company in a tough spot.

Other Harassment

The essence of policies around other harassment is that "Heck we were just joking around" is not an excuse for mistreating anyone. Often the focus is on harassment around ethnic origin (e.g. ethnic jokes), but the best path is simply to say that in our workplace we don't make fun of, demean, or harass anyone for any reason.

Set and enforce a high standard for polite professional behavior, and you'll avoid any complaints or lawsuits on harassment.

Areas Where You Have Less Power Than You Might Think

As a manager, you're the boss, right? Well, no, not really—not in the sense of what a boss is in cartoons or movies. For example, if an employee screws up, surely you can discipline them? Well, yes, but only within some strict constraints. Unless you happen to be in the Marines, you cannot tell an employee to give you ten push ups when they've underperformed. There are many guidelines that limit what you can do (check out your Employee Handbook). Okay, so that's the one lesson we really want to take away from this. You are not "the boss;" you are a manager in an organization that has a lot of rules. Let's look a little bit closer at what those rules are likely to be.

Disciplinary Actions: These need to be done with care. There must be a conclusive paper trail, documenting the need for the discipline. The disciplinary actions must not be excessive. The "time" must fit the "crime." These also must be done equitably for all offenders to maintain a just and fair process.

Termination: You must be in strict compliance with local, state, and federal laws to avoid "wrongful termination" litigation. So, you live in an "at will" employment state where you can fire for any or no reason, and likewise, an employee can resign for any or no reason, so you are good to go, right? Not so fast. If you should ever have to go to trial, juries are far more sympathetic to employees who were fired than to employers who did the firing. Here is where your justified and supported documentation of the legitimate causes for termination can be your best defense.

Policies You Need to Know Exist

If you are very eager, you've already opened up your employee handbook and started to memorize all the policies. We're not going to ask you to do that right now. The important thing is that you have a sense for where there are policies that you need to comply with, so that you look them up when the need arises. Here is a list:

- **Type of employee**. As a manager, your instinct may be to treat all of your workers the same way—we applaud that sentiment. However, there are different types of employment relationships such as exempt, non-exempt, part-time, contractor, and so on. If you give a part-time employee full-time hours, then that can affect their legal status and what benefits they are eligible for. If you invite a contractor to all your team parties, then that opens the door to a legal argument that they are really an employee not a contractor. You can ask an exempt employee to work late, but if you ask a non-exempt employee to do so, then you have to pay for that time—and potentially it's overtime. Make sure you know the type of employment status of each of the people working for you, and look up company policies that are relevant to each.

- **Flex Hours / Telecommuting.** Often as the manager, you can make your own decisions on who can telecommute and whether or not they need to keep strict office hours. Sometimes you cannot because there is a policy. You need to know what is allowed in your organization.

- **Leave.** There are many policies and regulations on leave. For example, the Family Medical and Leave Act (FMLA) has rules around the leave employees are entitled to for medical or family reasons. While you may have some flexibility on when you allow employees to take their leave, remember that many aspects are covered by laws or policies that you must comply with. Privacy laws under the FMLA, restrict an employer from revealing confidential medical information about the employee taking the leave. Any FMLA requests should be taken to the HR department to handle from the start.

- **Dress code.** There probably is a company dress code, and you may need to enforce it.

- **Employee privacy and work monitoring.** Generally, personal data about an employee must be kept private, and it's your duty to ensure that happens. However, you can monitor an employee's work, for example, recording business phone calls.

- **Social Media.** The laws and policies around social media are in flux. There is a tug of war between an employee's personal freedom and them taking action that can damage the reputation of their employer. You don't want to get into the middle of this one; pass any issues on to HR.

- **Expenses and Reimbursements:** Can your employee claim the cost of an umbrella as an expense when a rainstorm disrupts their business trip? Well, that's not up to you. Typically, companies have detailed policies on what can be claimed in expenses and reimbursements. Follow those policies.

This is not a comprehensive list but by now you have a sense of things. Policies and procedures are indeed pesky, but you must learn to comply.

Your Role in Enforcement

Remember, not only do you need to comply with policies and procedures, you are the "enforcer" who ensures employees comply as well. You need to educate your employees about the relevant policies. You need to enforce them with a firmness appropriate to the situation. At times, you'll need to involve HR. Don't overlook this important responsibility, as it's all part of being a manager.

Back to the Story

The company where Jeff and Jackie work has policies and procedures. These include fairly detailed expense reimbursement policies. The accounting clerk had checked, and expenses for arctic body scrubs were not covered.

Jackie didn't know what to tell Jeff. In the end she put it this way, "Jeff, it's your responsibility to know the relevant policies and procedures; and I guess it's my responsibility to make sure you know. I'm going to give you a break this time, because I know how hard you worked on that account." Then she handed him a personal check for the amount of the expenses. He had helped a key client and then had been a bit foolish. It was well worth it for her to eat that expense claim personally.

As Jeff walked out he gave a heartfelt thanks. Jackie said, "You're welcome, and next time, read the policies!"

Summing Up

Managers have many constraints on their behavior in the form of policies and procedures. There are usually good reasons for these policies, even if those reasons are not clear to you. In cases where the policy is based on legislative requirements, it is particularly important that you comply. Here are some of the key things you need to know:

- The EEOC exists to combat discrimination. Equal opportunity legislation has far-ranging implications. It all boils down to a need to be scrupulously fair to everyone on your team.

- Equal opportunity legislation is particularly challenging to comply with in interviews because many seemingly innocuous questions could uncover information (e.g. about their family or religion) that would open grounds for a discrimination suit. Follow HR's lead.

- The ADA requires you to make reasonable accommodations so that disabled employees can do their work. If someone asks for an accommodation, take that request seriously.

- FMLA has rules around leave that employees are entitled to for medical or family reasons.

- Sexual harassment is a serious issue with strict requirements. It's not about what you think is right or wrong but whether an employee feels sexually harassed. You have to set a high standard and enforce it.

- Any other kind of harassment is a major issue and, again, you have to set a high standard and enforce it.

- You have less power than you might think in terms of discipline, termination, and many other matters. Read the employee handbook and consult with HR whenever you are in doubt.

Alright, well that's a lot to think about. Now let's gather the team for an activity so you can learn about policies in your workplace.

Dig Up that Dusty Employee Handbook

In this chapter, we've often said you need to know the policies in your organization. Here's a useful practical exercise that will help you do just that.

- Schedule a 30-minute meeting for your team first thing on a Monday morning. Make sure there is coffee, and maybe snacks. Have a copy of the employee handbook for everyone.

- Tell them that you are going to work through this together – and though you might not get it all done today, you'll make a good start.

- Assign everyone 3 or 4 pages to read, and ask them to make notes in the form.

- After people have read their part, get each person to share the highlights.

- In closing, book a follow up session next month.

Employee Handbook Review		
Policies in my section that we should all know about	Idea in a nutshell	Consequences if we don't comply
Meal expenses	When we are on business travel, we can claim meal expenses but only to a certain limit, and we need to keep the receipts.	We won't be reimbursed.

WRAPPING IT UP

THE IDEAS THAT MATTER MOST

Key Terms and Definitions

Reflection - stopping to think about your work and what you've learned

The Issue

Being a manager is complex. We've covered a lot of topics. Now it's time to collect your thoughts and move forward.

A Short Story

This time, let's share a real story. It's about Bob Catell and Kenny Moore. Bob was CEO of KeySpan Energy in New York. Kenny was a former monk who had become his corporate ombudsman. Kenny's role was to bring the human, one might even say spiritual, side to the business. Bob, who was from an engineering background, recognized that Kenny had something unique to offer.

Kenny was famous in the organization for out-of-the-box thinking. As part of changing corporate culture, he held a funeral for the old culture; as a way to resolve an ongoing conflict between two managers, he had them read horoscopes; and to help his boss, CEO Bob Catell, became a better leader, Kenny told him to go and have lunch.

The lunch wasn't just any lunch. He told Bob he should be "breaking bread" with the common worker. Kenny advised the CEO to regularly have meals with small groups of his employees. This led Bob to wonder what he should be saying at these meals. Should he be sharing mission, vision, and values? Should he be helping them solve particular problems? No, Kenny advised that he shouldn't say anything at all; he should just sit and listen. [75]

Continuous learning as a manager is, in part, about being able to sit quietly and listen. That's a skill that made Bob Catell a great CEO. It's a skill that any manager can bring to their own work.

What Have We Covered?

Here's a list of the topics we have covered so far by section:

Section 1	Mission, Vision & Values Team-Strategic Alignment
Section 2	Diversity Inclusion
Section 3	Employment Branding Recruiting Candidate Experience
Section 4	Orientation and Onboarding Onboarding to Drive Productivity
Section 5	Compensation & Benefits Safety & Security
Section 6	Training Coaching Recognition
Section 7	Team Building Communications Performance Management
Section 8	Retention Employee Movement
Section 9	Policies & Procedures Wrap Up

That's a lot of content. One way to think about it is that your work as a manager follows a kind of sequence by:

- setting direction that aligns with the organization's mission, vision and values

- hiring people and bringing them on board

- ensuring they are paid

- developing and inspiring them

- developing a team

- developing and maintaining an inclusive culture

- following the rules

"First, set direction"

You might consider drawing a little diagram of how all of this fits together in a way that makes sense to you. After all, you are the one who needs to keep this straight, and that will be easier if you've explained it in your own words or pictures.

Here are a couple of examples of sketches others used to capture what mattered to them. Use your creativity to create an image that works for you.

Maria's Diagram

Set Direction

Include and comply

Team

Develop

Hire

Tom's Diagram

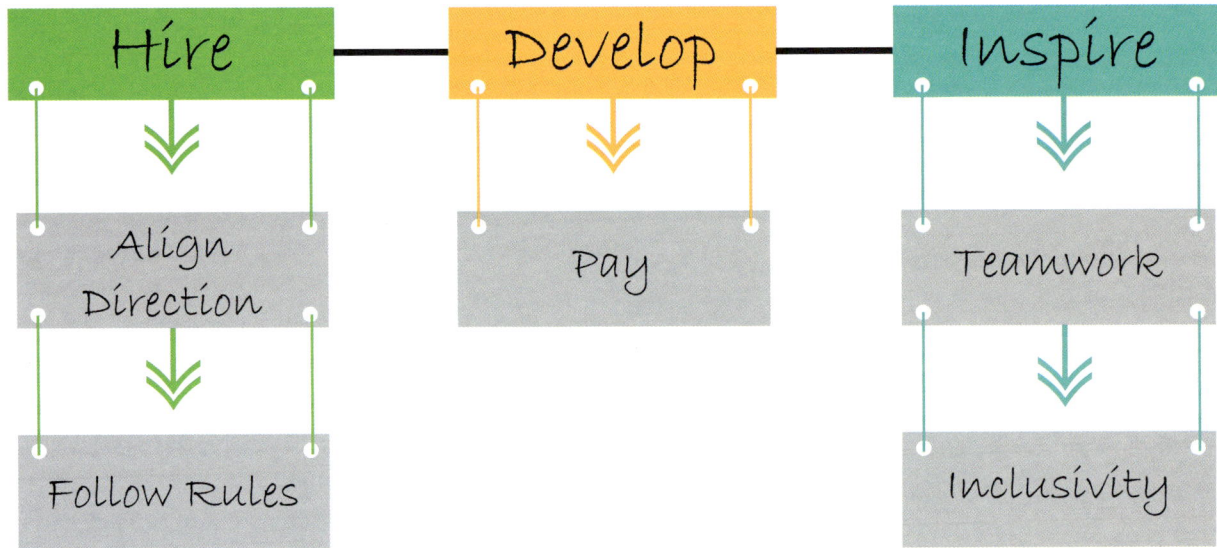

What Lessons Have We Learned?

In addition to all of the detailed content, are there some general lessons we've learned? Here's our view:

- **There are a lot of different elements to management**. Management has a much broader and more inherently chaotic set of responsibilities than most individual contributor jobs. The days when you could sit down and focus on just one thing are gone. You live in a world of multiple conflicting priorities and constant interruptions.

244

HR Fundamentals for Non-HR Managers: Can We Be Friends? (& CYA!)

"Empathy goes a long way."

- **Empathy goes a long way in getting the best from employees**. You can think about the specifics of communication or inclusion or recognition or motivation, but it is all rooted in your ability to see the world through the eyes of each individual employee. It's about empathy.

- **You are not just managing individuals**. In addition to individuals, you are managing your team, you are managing a culture, and you are working within the wider goals of the organization. You have to align and balance these different perspectives.

- **You can't just shoot from the hip**. Management is too complicated and regulations too pervasive to shoot from the hip. Your own gut feel isn't enough; you have to take a thoughtful and disciplined approach to your actions.

- **HR is a valuable partner**. There is a lot of help HR can provide with all the topics we've covered in this book. Get to know them, seek their insights, and learn the reasons behind their point of view.

- **It's no wonder that some managers are bad managers.** When you look at how challenging the role of a manager is, it's no wonder that there are some bad managers. You might also have realized some managers you thought were bad managers were just balancing a broader and more complex set of issues than you were aware of. Be gracious in judging others—all managers have flaws.

Those are some of the general lessons you might take away from this book. What's more interesting is what general lessons you *did* take away. What ideas resonated with you?

Partner with HR (and CYA)

Just do it!

> You can learn
> a lot from
> books.

Where Can You Learn More?

Next time you meet a more experienced manager, ask them at what point they felt they had management all figured out. We'll let them speak for themselves, but it's fair to say that never-ending learning is a big part of being an effective manager.

Most of the learning you get as a manager comes from experience. However, just because you are having experiences, doesn't mean you are learning from them. Dr. Henry Mintzberg of McGill University says, "Thoughtful reflection on natural experience, in the light of conceptual ideas is the most powerful tool we have for management learning." [76]

Reflection can be done in two ways. One way is when you are alone, maybe going for a walk, or in the shower, or sitting quietly with a coffee. You think about what's happening and try to make sense of it. The other way is through conversation; you sit down with someone and bounce your ideas off of them. Sometimes you are looking for a lot of input from them, but more often you just want a good listener. British novelist E.M. Forster said, "How do I know what I think until I see what I say?" [77] Managers can often relate to that. It's only after they try to articulate their ideas in a conversation with someone else that they truly understand their own ideas.

Let's be clear about the takeaway here. You *should* build time into your managerial life to reflect and talk about what is going on. It's important that you do so, and you'll find that this saves time, rather than take time because it gives you clarity about the situation and helps you learn lessons you can apply in the future.

The second part of Mintzberg's advice is reflecting on experience *"in light of a conceptual framework."* You can learn conceptual frameworks in three ways. The obvious way is through formal education via courses or books. This book has tried to introduce some frameworks that you can (so to speak) hang your experiences off of. For example, we talked about three reasons people might not be performing: lack of skill, lack of motivation, or lack of opportunity. As you reflect on what's happening in your own team, this framework might help you make sense of the situation. Another way to learn frameworks is to talk to other managers and ask them how they think through issues or if there are any frameworks they find helpful. Finally, you can come up with your own frameworks—just get out a pencil and sketch out some ideas. (Then refine them with a peer manager.)

We can also learn from the experience of others. Conversations with mentors are valuable. We might hope to find a mentor like Yoda from Star Wars who sees that we are special and devotes intense effort to our development. If this happens, we are very lucky, and may the force be with us. More likely, we simply need to seek out conversations with experienced managers wherever we find them. Mentors are everywhere, so seek them out. You can learn a lot by talking and LISTENING to your employees or peers or even Uber drivers!

There are endless opportunities to learn. Stay hungry for the lessons.

Back to the Story

KeySpan went on to become part of National Grid and Bob Catell became the chairman of the US operations. Kenny Moore retired. They wrote a book about their experiences together called, *"The CEO and the Monk: One Company's Journey to Profit and Purpose."* [78] Their actions didn't follow a playbook. It followed a deep understanding of human nature. Continuous learning as a manager will rely on ever deeper insight into how humans can work together in the strange world of organizations.

Summing Up

Let's sum up with three broad ideas that will help in your career as a manager.

- There are a very wide range of responsibilities, rules, ideas, and tactics you need to know as a manager.

- As a general principle, being able to see the world through your employees' eyes will help you be a more effective manager.

- You should devote considerable time to learning throughout your career as a manager. This isn't so much about taking courses at university as it is about taking time to read, reflect, converse, and listen.

It's time for one last activity.

Why I Wanted to Be a Manager and Why I Still Do

Can you remember when you first thought about becoming a manager? When did you first think it might be for you? In the exercise below, you'll explore what being a manager means to you. We hope you will be inspired by the importance of the role.

- Start by writing three to five reasons why you originally wanted to be a manager (column 1); be brutally honest.
- Next, write out whether those reasons proved to be valid now that you have experience managing (column 2).
- Finally, write three to five reasons why you still want to be a manager (column 3).

(Let's hope you have so many reasons that they won't fit in this table.)

Why I originally wanted to be a manager	How that original reason has panned out in practice.	Why I still want to be a manager

Okay, now go out and become the manager you aspire to be!

248

HR Fundamentals for Non-HR Managers: Can We Be Friends? (& CYA!)

SUMMARY

> **Well done is better than well said**
> – Benjamin Franklin

Management involves an astonishingly wide range of skills. In this book we've focused on the skills relevant to people management. We have also emphasized how to align with your HR department. HR can be a great friend in helping you get the most from your people. They can also help you keep out of trouble. Let's take a look at what we have covered throughout this guide:

Section One: *Being a Strategic Leader: Aligning your team with the bigger picture*

This section challenged you to strategically align yourself and your team to the mission, vision, and values of the company. Doing so will keep you focused on what most matters to the organization.

Section Two: *Creating a Respectful Environment: Improving diversity, equity, and inclusion on your team*

Defining and understanding diversity, equity, and inclusion is integral to creating, engaging, and managing a cross-cultural team. Make sure you get input from your team on how to best engage, since you may have blind spots concerning unconscious biases! Yeah, we didn't see those either!

Section Three: *Hook, Line, and Sinker: Catching the best talent*

You're the boss when it comes to recruiting and hiring for your team! Compliant, fair, and unbiased processes save time and money, and optimize results. In other words, do it right the first time around!

Section Four: *Onboarding and Orientation: You've got one chance to make a first impression*

Orientation is usually done by HR, but onboarding your team member is on your docket! First, get them set up and make them feel welcome. Next launch them to success by communicating clear goals and giving them the support they need! Go team!

Section Five: *Pay Day and the Safe Workplace: Handling compensation, safety, and security*

Money is a big deal and as a manager you need to know all about how compensation works in your organization. Once you have attracted and retained a strong team (thanks to effective pay policies), you'll want to keep them safe and secure. You need to know your role in maintaining safety and security.

Section Six: *Train, Coach & Inspire: Turn raw talent into real results*

You are the coach of your team, and this means more than just "spring training!" It requires learning the strengths and weaknesses of your team members, and ensuring they receive effective training to hone their expertise, and bolster what needs enhancement. Discovering and developing a career path that is beneficial to both the team member and the company is essential to growing both! Make sure your coaching includes a good deal of encouragement, recognize their accomplishments, and appreciate their efforts.

Section Seven: *Leading Your Team Doesn't Have To Be Like Herding Cats!*

Trust is the foundation upon which you will need to build your team. Start there and then apply your knowledge of team dynamics to help them perform. Keep them informed with good communication. Keep yourself informed with good listening. And keep everyone on track with agile performance management. Go, coach, go!

Section Eight: *Retention and Mobility: Making all the right moves*

"If you build it, they will come," but how do you build it so they will stay? Retaining your teams requires a range of tactics that you, as a savvy manager, employ to make people want to work for you. Of course, no one should stay on your team forever. You have to enable movement up, laterally, and out. Do it right!

Section Nine: *The "Love to Hate" Policies and a Review of Core Concepts*

Oh, those policies and procedures! Being compliant with company regulations, national and regional laws is, once again, on your plate! No nail-biting needed. There are many ways to become aware and mindful of managing the team with competence, compliance, care, and consideration. But enough of the hard stuff. Take some time to reflect on what you learn and to consider how you'll continue to learn as a manager. We believe in you! You got this, right?!

We hope you picked up many people management tips that you can apply in your work. Applying the tips will help you create an effective team and an effective team will make your life much easier. If you invest in developing your skills in managing the people side of the business and in partnering with HR, you will find it pays off many times over.

END NOTES

1 Southwest Airlines. (2020). *Purpose, Vision, Values, and Mission*. Retrieved from http://investors.southwest.com/our-company/purpose-vision-values-and-mission

2 The Princess Margaret Cancer Foundation. (2020). *Vision, Mission & Strategy*. Retrieved from https://thepmcf.ca/About-Us/About-the-Foundation/Vision-Mission-Strategy

3 Johnson, A. (n.d.). *How to get employees to align with the company's mission*. Retrieved from https://www.bizjournals.com/bizjournals/how-to/growth-strategies/2014/06/how-to-get-employees-to-align-with-company-mission.html

4 Clifton, J., & Harter, J. K. (2019). *It's the Manager: Gallup finds the quality of managers and team leaders is the single biggest factor in your organization's long-term success*. New York, NY: Gallup Press.

5 Johnson, A. (n.d.). *How to get employees to align with the company's mission*. Retrieved from https://www.bizjournals.com/bizjournals/how-to/growth-strategies/2014/06/how-to-get-employees-to-align-with-company-mission.html

6 Browne, S. (2019, January 2). *HR Roundtable: What is Culture?* Retrieved from https://www.tlnt.com/hr-roundtable-what-is-culture/

7 Clifton, J., & Harter, J. K. (2019). *It's the Manager: Gallup finds the quality of managers and team leaders is the single biggest factor in your organizations long-term success*. New York, NY: Gallup Press.

8 Browne, S. (2019, January 2). *HR Roundtable: What is Culture?* Retrieved from https://www.tlnt.com/hr-roundtable-what-is-culture/

9 Sinek, S. (n.d.). *Start with Why: How Great Leaders Inspire Action*. Retrieved from https://www.ted.com/talks/simon_sinek_how_great_leaders_inspire_action?language=en#t-6873

10 Thomas, R. (2018, October 30). *The First Step to Great Leadership is Self-Awareness*. Retrieved from https://www.tlnt.com/the-first-step-to-great-leadership-is-self-awareness/

11 Larkin, B. (2019, July 18). *30 Craziest Corporate Policies Employees Must Follow*. Retrieved from https://bestlifeonline.com/craziest-corporate-policies-employees-must-adhere-to/

12 Clemmer, J. (n.d.). *Stop Whining and Start Leading. (n.d.)*. Retrieved from https://www.clemmergroup.com/articles/stop-whining-start-leading/

13 Rock, D. (2009, August 27). *Managing with the Brain in Mind*. Retrieved from https://www.strategy-business.com/article/09306?gko=5df7f

14 Thomas, R. (2019, April 16). *The Two Most Powerful Leadership Phrases*. Retrieved from https://www.tlnt.com/the-two-most-powerful-leadership-phrases/

15 Clifton, J., & Harter, J. K. (2019). *It's the Manager: Gallup finds the quality of managers and team leaders is the single biggest factor in your organizations long-term success*. New York, NY: Gallup Press.

16 University of Oregon at Gladstone. *Definition of Diversity*. (n.d.). Retrieved from https://gladstone.uoregon.edu/~asuomca/diversityinit/definition.html

17 Limeade Marketing. (2019, February 28). *The Guide to Inclusion in Your Workplace*. Retrieved from https://www.limeade.com/2019/02/the-guide-to-inclusion-in-your-workplace/

18 Johnson, S. (2019). *The Advantages of Equity in the Workplace*. Retrieved from https://work.chron.com/advantages-equity-workplace-2635.html

19 Clifton, J. K., & Harter, J. K. (2019). *It's the Manager: Gallup finds the quality of managers and team leaders is the single biggest factor in your organization's long-term success*. New York, NY: Gallup Press.

20 Limeade Marketing. (2019, February 28). *The Guide to Inclusion in Your Workplace*. Retrieved from https://www.limeade.com/2019/02/the-guide-to-inclusion-in-your-workplace/

21 Footnote (new) Acecqa. (2016, July 13). *What does it mean to be culturally competent?* Retrieved from https://wehearyou.acecqa.gov.au/2014/07/10/what-does-it-mean-to-be-culturally-competent/#_ftnref3

22 Rock, D. (2009, August 27). *Managing with the Brain Mind.* Retrieved from https://www.strategy-business.com/article/09306?gko=5df7f

23 King, C. (2019). *How to Manage a Diverse Team.* Retrieved from https://www.webucator.com/how-to/how-manage-diverse-team.cfm

24 Medlin, D. (2019, July 19) *Whole-Person Hiring: What's Next in Talent Acquisition.* Retrieved from https://blog.proactivetalent.com/whole-person-hiring-whats-next-in-talent-acquisition

25 Hudson, K. (2019, March 29). *Why Employer Branding is Critical in Attracting Top Talent.* Retrieved from https://www.jobvite.com/employment-branding/why-employer-branding-is-critical-in-attracting-top-talent/

26 Clifton, J., & Harter, J. K. (2019). *It's the Manager: Gallup finds the quality of managers and team leaders is the single biggest factor in your organization's long-term success.* New York, NY: Gallup Press.

27 TalentLyft. (2019). *Candidate Engagement Definition.* Retrieved from https://www.talentlyft.com/en/resources/what-is-candidate-engagement

28 ClearCompany. (2019, August). *Create an Awesome Onboarding Experience with the Best of ClearCompany.* Retrieved from https://blog.clearcompany.com/create-awesome-onboarding-experience-best-clearcompany

29 Maurer, R. (2018, February 23). *Employers Risk Driving New Hires Away with Poor Onboarding.* Retrieved from https://www.shrm.org/resourcesandtools/hr-topics/talent-acquisition/pages/employers-nEw-hires-poor-onboarding.aspx

30 Clifton, J. K., & Harter, J. K. (2019). *It's the Manager: Gallup finds the quality of managers and team leaders is the single biggest factor in your organization's long-term success.* New York, NY: Gallup Press.

31 Kearl, B. (2018, August 20). *The Onboarding Checklist That Puts Culture First.* Retrieved from https://www.glassdoor.com/employers/blog/onboarding-checklist-culture/

32 de Luca, R. (2018, December 14). *Creative Ways to Keep Remote Employees Engaged.* Retrieved from https://www.bamboohr.com/blog/creative-ways-to-keep-remote-employees-engaged/

33 Myhre, J. (2019, March 8). *Why New-Hire Onboarding Fails and How You Can Make It a Success.* Retrieved from www.flimp.net/why-new-hire-onboarding-fails-and-how-you-can-make-it-a-success/

34 Wallace, W. (2019). *You can't know it all: leading in the age of deep expertise.* New York: Harper Business.

35 DigitalHR. (2019). *How Career Pathing Can Help You Win Talent and Boost Engagement.* Retrieved from https://www.digitalhrtech.com/career-pathing/

36 Business News Daily. (2019). *6 Benefits That Attract Top Talent.* Retrieved from https://www.businessnewsdaily.com/11204-top-benefits-attract-top-talent.html

37 Haden, J. (2012). *How to Make the Perfect Job Offer: 9 Tips.* Retrieved from https://www.inc.com/jeff-haden/how-to-make-the-perfect-job-offer-9-tips.html

38 Bureau of Labor Statistics. (2019). Retrieved from https://www.bls.gov/

39 National Safety Council. (n.d.). *Drivers are Falling Asleep Behind the Wheel.* Retrieved from https://www.nsc.org/road-safety/safety-topics/fatigued-driving

40 Weick, K. E. (2007). *Managing the unexpected: resilient performance in an age of uncertainty.* San Francisco, CA: Jossey-Bass.

41 AMTrust Financial. (2019). *ROI of Safety: How to Create a Long-Term Profitable Workplace Safety Program.* Retrieved from https://amtrustfinancial.com/resource-center/trends-and-research/roi-of-safety?fbclid=

252

HR Fundamentals for Non-HR Managers: Can We Be Friends? (& CYA!)

42 Hallenbeck, et. al. (2011). *The Seven Faces of Learning Agility*. Retrieved from https://www.kornferry.com/media/lominger_pdf/Seven_faces_of_learning_agility.pdf

43 Harkavy, D., & Halliday, S. (2010). Becoming a Coaching Leader: The proven strategy for building your own team of champions

44 Clifton, J., & Harter, J. (2019). *It's The Manager: Gallup finds that the quality of managers and team leaders is the single biggest factor in your organization's long-term success.* New York, NY: Gallup Press.

45 Goldsmith, M., & Lyons, L. (2005). *Coaching for Leadership: The Practice of Leadership Coaching from the World's Greatest Coaches.* Pfeiffer.

46 Coach U Inc. (2005). *The Coach U Personal and Corporate Coach Training Handbook.* Hoboken, N.J: Wiley.

47 Clifton, J., & Harter, J. (2019). *It's The Manager: Gallup finds that the quality of managers and team leaders is the single biggest factor in your organization's long-term success.* New York, NY: Gallup Press.

48 Elton, C. (2020, April 29). Personal interview.

49 Agovino, T. (2019, August 16). *Building Team Bonds*. Retrieved from https://www.shrm.org/hr-today/news/all-things-work/pages/building-team-bonds.aspx

50 Lencioni. P. (2002). *The Five Dysfunctions of a Team.* Jossey-Bass.

51 Tuckman, B. (1965). *Developmental sequence in small groups. Psychological Bulletin.* Retrieved 2008-11-10. "Reprinted with permission in Group Facilitation, Spring 2001".

52 Scott, D. H. (2011, January 6). *Understanding Recent Family Functions – And Applying Our "Stages of Group Development Learning" to Business.* Retrieved from http://learningpursuits.com/understanding-recent-family-functions-and-applying-our-stages-of-group-development-learning-to-business/

53 Based on: Argyris, C. (1990). *Overcoming Organizational Defenses: Facilitating Organizational Learning*, 1st Edition. Copyright 1990.

54 Scott, D. H. (2011, January 6). *Understanding Recent Family Functions – And Applying Our "Stages of Group Development Learning" to Business.* Retrieved from http://learningpursuits.com/understanding-recent-family-functions-and-applying-our-stages-of-group-development-learning-to-business/

55 Senge, P. M., Kleiner, A., Roberts, C., Ross, R. R., & Smith, B. J. (1994). *The fifth discipline fieldbook: Strategies and tools for building a learning organization.* New York: Currency Doubleday.

56 Sherf, Tangirala, Venkataramani. (2019, April 8). *Harvard Business Review. Research: Why Managers Ignore Employees' Ideas.* Retrieved from https://hbr.org/2019/04/research-why-managers-ignore-employees-ideas

57 Reynolds, J. (2016, October 6). *The Importance of Ongoing Feedback for Performance Management.* Retrieved from https://www.tinypulse.com/blog/ongoing-feedback-performance-management

58 HR.com's HR Research Institute. (2019). *The State of Performance Management 2019.*

59 BambooHR. (2019). *Performance Management.* Retrieved from https://www.bamboohr.com/hr-glossary/performance-management/

60 Hassell, D. (2018, March 15). *5 Lessons To Align Your Team And Achieve Superior Results.* Retrieved from https://www.15five.com/blog/5-lessons-to-align-your-team/

61 HR.com's HR Research Institute. (2019). *The State of Performance Management 2019.*

62 HR.com's HR Research Institute. (2019). *The State of Performance Management 2019*.

63 Reynolds, J. (2016, October 6). *The Importance of Ongoing Feedback for Performance Management*. Retrieved from https://www.tinypulse.com/blog/ongoing-feedback-performance-management

64 ClearCompany. (2019). *A Manager's Guide to Giving Effective Performance Feedback*. Retrieved from https://offers.clearcompany.com/guide-effective-feedback-performance

65 Psychometrics.com. (2019). *The True Cost of Employee Turnover*. Retrieved from https://www.psychometrics.com/true-cost-employee-turnover/

66 Adams, B. (2019, December 10). *This Avoidable Situation is Costing U.S. Business $11 Billion Every Single Year*. Retrieved from https://www.inc.com/bryan-adams/this-avoidable-situation-is-costing-us-businesses-11-billion-every-single-year.html

67 Wright, H. (2016, March 23). *What Crazy Quitting Stories Can Teach You about Employee Retention*. Retrieved from https://www.quantumworkplace.com/future-of-work/what-crazy-quitting-stories-can-teach-you-about-employee-retention

68 Wronski, L. (2019). *CNBC|SurveyMonkey Workplace Happiness Index: July 2019*. Retrieved from https://www.surveymonkey.com/curiosity/cnbc-workplace-happiness-index-july-2019/

69 Work Institute. (2018). *2018 RETENTION REPORT Truth & Trends in Turnover*.

70 Gostick, A. R., & Elton, C. (2020). *Leading with gratitude: eight leadership practices for extraordinary business results*. New York, NY: Harper Business, an imprint of HarperCollins Publishers.

71 Ulrich, D., & Ulrich, W. (2010). *The Why of Work: How great leaders build abundant organizations that win*. Maidenhead: McGraw-Hill.

72 Buckingham, M. (2006). *The one thing you need to know about great managing, great leading, and sustained individual success*. London: Pocket Books.

73 Clifton, J., & Harter, J. K. (2019). *It's the Manager: Gallup finds the quality of managers and team leaders is the single biggest factor in your organization's long-term success*. New York, NY: Gallup Press

74 SHRM. (2018, June 11). *Equal Employment Opportunity Policy: Basic*. Retrieve from https://www.shrm.org/resourcesandtools/tools-and-samples/policies/pages/cms_005022.aspx

75 Catell, R. & Moore, K. (2004). *The CEO and the Monk: One Company's Journey to Profit and Purpose*. John Wiley & Sons.

76 Coaching Ourselves. (2020). *Mintzberg and LeNir's approach to developing leaders is 70:20:10 all in one*. Retrieved from https://coachingourselves.com/mintzberg-and-lenirs-approach-to-developing-leaders-is-702010-all-in-one/

77 Forster, E.M. (2019). *How Can I Know What I Think Till I See What I Say?* Quote Investigator. Retrieved from https://quoteinvestigator.com/2019/12/11/know-say/

78 Catell, R. B., Moore, K., & Rifkin, G. (2004). *The CEO and the Monk: One Company's Journey to Profit and Purpose*. John Wiley & Sons.

254

HR Fundamentals for Non-HR Managers: Can We Be Friends? (& CYA!)